BLOOD BROTHER

Israel's Ancient Enemy

James Donald Long

Lightcatcher Books
Springdale, AR

BLOOD BROTHER
Israel's Ancient Enemy

James Donald Long

© 2011, all rights reserved

ISBN 13: 978-0-9792618-5-5
ISBN 10: 0-9792618-5-6

Biblical History/Philosophy/Geo-Politics

No part of this book may be reproduced or transmitted in any form or by any means, electronic or mechanical, including photocopying, recording, or by any information storage and retrieval system, without permission in writing from the publisher, except in the case of brief quotations in reviews for inclusion in a magazine, newspaper or broadcast.

Published by Lightcatcher Books, printed in the United States of America and Israel

1204 Kissinger Ave.
Springdale, AR 72762
lightcatcherbooks.com

Cover Art: Carol Long

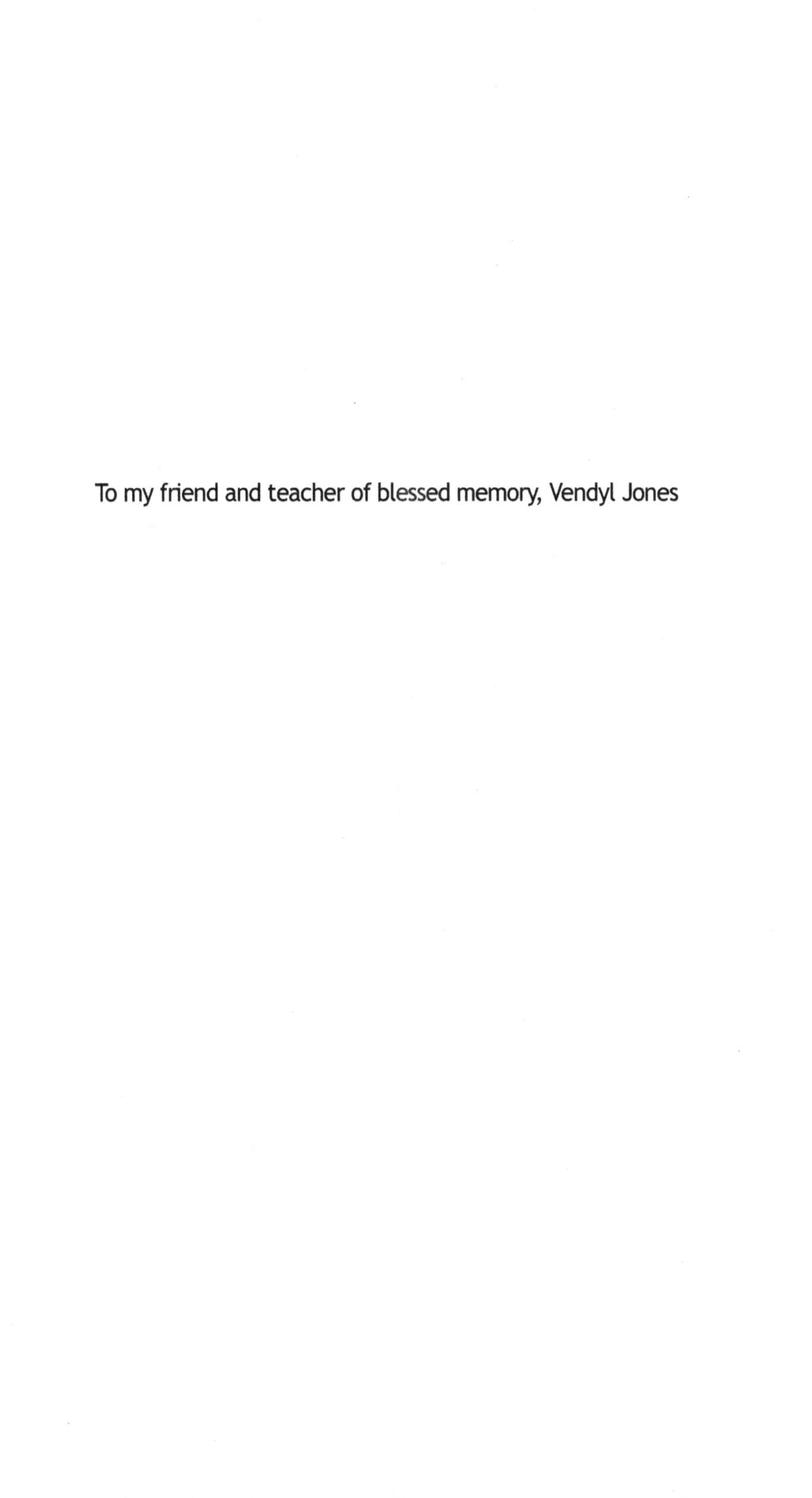

To my friend and teacher of blessed memory, Vendyl Jones

TABLE OF CONTENTS

Chapter One

TRAGEDY AND HOPE

> Was not Esau Jacob's brother? saith HaShem; yet I loved Jacob; But Esau I hated...
>
> — Malachi 1:2

Why does G-d hate Esau?

Genesis 36:1 identifies Esau's offspring collectively as Edom. The meaning of Edom is red – hinting of the blood that would be spilled pursuing his desire to dominate Jacob and his descendants. The formative experiences of the Jewish People are rooted in an epic, centuries-long wrestling match that began with the birth of Jacob and Esau. Just as Jacob stood opposite his brother Esau and beheld his own rough reflection, the civilizations that sprang from these two still oppose one another while exhibiting similar aspects.

The Jewish sages believed that Edom was Rome, the foundation of our modern Western World and Christianity. Classical Roman ideas of culture, commerce and government are rooted in Edom. But those roots are more than just philosophical. The actual origins of Rome, as we will demonstrate in these pages, can be traced legitimately – even ethnically – to Biblical Esau/Edom. These connections can be found in the *Tanakh* as well as the rich Oral Tradition as preserved in the *Talmud* and *Midrash*. As we examine the eternal struggle between Jacob and Esau, we will also introduce textual and physical evidence from history, linguistics and archaeology.

As we probe the roots of this conflict, we will look to both the Written and the Oral Torah. For the Torah-observant Jew, it is an article of faith that the Creator gave the *Torah She-b'al Peh* (Oral Torah) to Moses on Mount Sinai. I can use limited contemporary parlance and liken it to a kind of lecture but describing it in this manner only diminishes what was surely the most splendid communication ever experienced by any single human being. It was a unique moment in the history of the world.

That hallowed discourse was presented to Moses during three sessions eventually totaling 120 days. However, the words of Torah were not written down until the end of his life, at the age of 120. The written text only provides the basics of the Creator's instructions to the nation of Israel. The Oral Torah encompasses and preserves the existential principles necessary for insuring continuity of the Divine plan and the people who accepted the task of implementing it.

> If the entire Torah would have been given in writing, everyone would be able to interpret it as he desired. This would lead to division and discord among people who followed Torah in different ways. The Oral Torah, on the other hand, would require a central authority to preserve it, thus assuring the unity of Israel.
>
> — Rabbi Aryeh Kaplan[1]

We cannot hope to grasp the depth of the Written Torah without its Oral counterpart. After all, Torah means *instruction*, which is only effective through the vibrant teacher-pupil relationship. In essence, you can read a text all day long, but it is only through the faculty of speech that words come to life. That divine faculty resonates most profoundly with Moses' final words to the Israelites. Prior to their entry into the Promised Land, he taught an extraordinary song to the assembled tribes. The song is the Oral Torah.

---

[1] Rabbi Aryeh Kaplan, *Handbook of Jewish Thought*, Vol. 1 (Moznaim Publishing, Brooklyn, NY, 1992) p. 179

> Now write for yourselves this song and teach it to the Israelites. Make them memorize it, so that this song will be a witness for the Israelites.
>
> – Deuteronomy 31:19

The above verse is also the source for the commandment that requires every Jewish male to either write his own complete Torah Scroll or have one written for him.

When it was time to bequeath the mantle of leadership, Moses taught the entire Torah to Joshua who later instructed Elazar, who then passed it on to Pinchas. It was Pinchas who taught the elders of Israel. It was in this manner that the entire Torah was transmitted through the centuries, amid war and wandering. Through these trials it was probed, dissected, and written down in the academies of Yavneh, as the *Mishna*. In that form it was further explored and codified as the *Talmud* some three hundred years later in the Jewish learning centers of Babylon. Though the Talmudists recorded this compendium of sacred instruction, they believed that oral transmission was still superior to the written word.

There are those who denigrate the Oral Torah and brand it a rabbinic invention used to lure people away from the truth. That attitude ignores an exhaustively explored G-d-given resource that can be traced, year by year, from the completion of the Talmud by Rabbi Ashi, Ravina and others in the Hebrew year 4260 – all the way back to the year 2448 and the giving of the Torah at Mount Sinai.[2]

Rejecting the Oral Torah is tantamount to walking away from a lively discussion between some of the world's most gifted minds and ultimately shunning the revelatory rewards of the Torah. Worst of all, it is denying an authoritative body of applied wisdom from the very people who understand it in

---

[2] The list of those who passed the Oral Torah down through the centuries is still known to the Jewish People. See *Forty Centuries-Milestones in Early Jewish History* (Kehot Publication Society, Brooklyn, NY, 1998) p. 19

the original language in which it was transmitted with context and nuance intact.

The attitude of those who arbitrarily decide the Oral Torah is some pious fraud is mystifying. Imagine a scholar from earth meeting an alien from another planet who arrives with a text book written in his own alien tongue. The scholar has never been to the planet and barely speaks the alien tongue, yet he feels compelled to describe to the alien, life on that planet. Then the earthling attempts to interpret the alien textbook for the alien. The analogy may be clumsy but you get my point.

In the rather narrow scope of this book, we will not only look at the text of the Torah but explore the meaning embedded within the Hebrew names and places. In addition to revealing personal attributes, names in the Torah are also a prophetic depiction of the era in which these figures lived and died. The most obvious example can be found in Genesis 10:25: *And to Eber was born two sons: one was named Peleg, because in his days the earth was divided.*

The root of the name Peleg denotes division or fracturing.[3] Peleg witnessed massive seismic activity that rocked the earth. Eventually, at the end of Peleg's life, the tectonic plates of the planet shifted apart. That catastrophic global shift destroyed the Tower of Babel and separated people into distinct languages and nations. In every sense, the earth and its people were truly divided.

The Hebrew language of the Torah is also a window into the past. We will see how contemporary words and even geographic designations contain Hebraic links to antiquity. For instance, the name for the ancient city of **Rome**, famous

[3] Isaac Mozeson, *The Origin of Speeches*, 2nd Edition (Lightcatcher Books / Springdale, AR / 2011)

for being built on seven hills, sounds very much like the Hebrew word *ram* which means lofty. A quiet neighborhood established on one of the elevated districts of Jerusalem is called **Rome**ma. The plural form of the root is given to the communities in Israel built in the heights such as **Ram**ot or **Ram**at Beit Shemesh.

The reader will also encounter another prophetic mode expressed as *Ma'asei Avot siman la-banim* or "the experiences of the Patriarchs foreshadow the experiences of their descendants."[4]

In a lesser degree, we can see this at work in other nations of antiquity. They are distinguished by their culture and traditions derived from the way they respond to the world around them. Their general behavior is an expression of the experiences of their founding families. For Israel, it is even more striking. An illustration of this principle is the story of Abraham and Sarah's migration to Egypt during a wide-spread famine. When they arrived at the borders of Egypt Sarah was taken captive and held by the pharaoh. During her stay in the palace, the entire royal entourage was struck with physical disorders. The king eventually realized that his actions precipitated the plague. A relieved king released Abraham and Sarah. They departed the country laden with royal gifts. This event presages the experiences of Abraham's descendants, the Twelve Tribes. A famine also forced them to journey to Egypt. Years later they departed in the wake of terrible plagues – showered with riches by the Egyptians.[5]

Another example is the story of Hagar, the Egyptian, who joined the household of Abraham and later became a source

[4] Rabbi Moshe Ben Nachman, aka the Ramban (1194-c. 1270)

[5] Exodus 3:22 and Exodus 12:35-36

of terrible discord in the family. That episode was replicated by the Egyptians who joined the Israelites at the time of the Exodus. Many of them were part of a tragic rebellion that resulted in the Sin of the Golden Calf.[6] It should be noted that not every Egyptian did so. Notably, I Chronicles 4:17-18 states that pharaoh's daughter married a man from the tribe of Judah named Mered.

The model of *Ma'asei Avot siman la-banim* permeates the history of the Jewish People. Individually and collectively they have continually responded to a delicate circuitry etched into their psyche by the powerful experiences of their spiritually elevated ancestors. This idea does not negate the principle of Free Will but rather reveals a mysterious process that allows the Chosen People to find their way through history and, when necessary, back onto the path to their ultimate mission – to bring the entire world to the awareness of the one true G-d.

Despite having parents whose lives were infused with belief in the plan that the Creator has for humankind, Esau chose to reject the plan. He and his offspring would enforce his own opposing philosophy with the sword. Meanwhile, his brother Jacob embraced all that Isaac and Rebecca held sacred. These two world views have nurtured the political and religious underpinnings of whole cultures and is the source of a centuries-long clash of civilizations. This is a classic saga of brother pitted against brother that began with their birth just over three thousand, six hundred years ago.[7]

---

[6] Known collectively as the *Erev Rav*, they are blamed for fomenting a revolt that led to the Sin of the Golden Calf at Mt. Sinai.

[7] The calculation is derived from *Seder HaOlam*, the Jewish chronology which counts the years from the creation of Adam. Jacob and Esau were born 2,108 years after Adam.

The troublesome legacy of Esau flourished throughout history and provided the ideological fuel that powered world conquests. The clash between Jacob and Esau was apparent even as they were formed in the womb of their mother Rebecca.

Chapter Two

BIRTH OF A NATION

The Jewish Oral Tradition relates that in the seventh month of Rebecca's pregnancy, her contractions were so violent that she asked other women if they had experienced anything similar. The new mother was distressed and felt she might be unable to survive the birth. Rebecca sought counsel from her revered father-in-law, Abraham.[8] The sages teach that she also consulted Shem and Ever. Shem, the son of Noah, bore the title of *Melchizedek*. He was the custodian of the holy wisdom preserved and passed down from Noah, his father.[9]

The Creator, spoke to Rebecca through these prophets:

> Two nations are in thy womb, and two manners of people shall be separated from thy bowels; and the one people shall be stronger than the other people; and the elder shall serve the younger.
>
> — Genesis 25:23

In the text of the above verse, the word for "nations" is translated from the Hebrew word *goyim*. Usually it is spelled with a *vav* (ו) but the text employs two *yuds* (hh - as if to represent twins) altering the word to read *geyim*, which denotes lofty ones or nobles.

G-d told Rebecca that world leaders would descend from the

[8] Rashi. Also see *Sefer HaYashar* 26:10-11

[9] *Midrash Rabbah* 63:6 on *Toledoth* (Volume II / The Socino Press/ London, New York) p. 561

two infants.[10]

As the twins tumbled out of the birth canal, Esau emerged ruddy and matted in a mantle of hair. The specifics of his physical traits are something rare in the Torah. Even someone as significant as Moses is never actually described, except for his speech impediment. When such details are revealed in the Torah – as in the case of Esau – they are particularly relevant. This rare expression of physical attributes of an individual is an indication that his very existence would be fueled by his bodily appetites.

We hear so much about the differences in the brothers that we might think that they bore no resemblance to one another. According to Rabbi Samson Raphael Hirsch, they were actually identical in appearance and are described in the text as *teomim*, or twins. Esau possessed a robust physical aspect, otherwise they resembled each other.[11] The name of Esau is derived from *asah* meaning "complete," a prophetic portent of his acutely independent nature. Esau did not need anything from anyone. He embraced this quality and reveled in the idea that he was a self-made man.

> The boys grew up. Esau became a skilled trapper, a man of the field. Jacob was a single-minded man, who lived in tents.
>
> – Genesis 25:27

When the lads reached the age of thirteen, their true natures emerged. Jacob was well disposed towards his elders. He was drawn to home and hearth, spending time

---

[10] Rabbi Yaakov Culi, *The Torah Anthology (MeAm Lo'ez)* Book Two translated by Rabbi Aryeh Kaplan (Moznaim Publishing, NY/Jerusalem 1989) p. 456

[11] *The Hirsch Chumash / Sefer Bereshis*, translated by Daniel Haberman (Feldheim/ Judaica Press / Jerusalem, New York 2002) p. 556

with those whose years had instilled them with wisdom. Esau was the restless, active son who became "a trapper with his mouth." There is an added layer of meaning found in these words. In addition to pleasing his father with the pursuit and preparation of wild game, he also distracted Isaac by engaging in pious discussions that were mere pretense on the part of Esau.

The Torah honestly portrays the strengths and the weaknesses of heroes, as well as villains. As we shall see, Jacob was just as capable of guile and deceit. However, the Torah offers a fundamental lesson in how each brother eventually dealt with their negative traits.

Isaac and Rebecca were righteous people but made two fundamental mistakes in the rearing of their sons. Their first error was to educate them in the very same manner, without regard to their natural tendencies. While Jacob was drawn to the study bench, Esau felt bridled and restrained having to learn in the same fashion as his sibling. Secondly, Isaac and Rebecca erred in their affection for the boys. They did not love them in equal measure. While Isaac was drawn to Esau's vitality, Rebecca found Jacob's quiet nobility more appealing. Her love was constant, as reflected in the literal rendering of Genesis 25:28, "...Rebecca favors Jacob." This could have been the motivation for the hatred Esau felt for his mother. The sages tell us that Esau considered killing Rebecca! His deep hostility extended to all women and would ultimately manifest itself in a rampage of murder, adultery and rape.[12]

By the time the boys were fifteen years of age they experienced a series of crucial episodes that significantly shaped their future as well as the destiny of their

---

[12] Rabbi Matis Weinberg, *Frameworks: Genesis* (Foundation for Jewish Publications / Boston, Jerusalem 1999) p. 145

descendants. The first pivotal turn in the family drama occurred with the sale of Esau's birthright for pottage. A superficial reading of this brief passage seems to offer little explanation, but that is exactly why the account is so spare. The lack of detail is symbolic of Esau's fleeting interest in the transaction. He just didn't give it much thought.

Why did Esau have so little regard for something his brother saw as valuable?

To discover the answer we must return to the very beginnings of humankind and the events that lead up to the sale. It is in these accounts that we find the seeds of Esau's fatal flaws of misplaced rage and unrestrained passions. We have to return to the Garden.

Chapter Three

MAN BECOMES A CONSUMER

The literal meaning of the word Torah is "instruction." By constantly keeping that as our frame of reference, we can understand why the drama of mankind unfolds in the Torah in the manner that it does. It is not simply history that we are reading. Indeed, the Jewish sages warn that even though Torah and the events recounted in its pages are truth, events are not always revealed in chronological order.

Film audiences are familiar with the cinematic device, known as a flashback, in which the action shifts back in time to clarify a story point. The Torah sometimes will relate an incident out of chronological order to connect and deepen its context with another event. In certain instances, details are rendered in richly symbolic language. This is most apparent in the creation account and subsequently in the narrative of Adam and Eve. The method in which their story is told enables us to absorb the details as pure instruction.

Things go awry when Adam and Eve transgress by eating from the Tree of the Knowledge of Good and Evil. They had failed their first test. In his evocative commentary on Genesis 3:1, Rav Hirsch startles us with this shattering assessment:

> The logic of an animal persuaded the first man to deviate from the path of duty; today this same animal logic still serves as a midwife to all human sin.[13]

Even though the Creator sent an agent to test Adam and Eve, the *naHash* is also culpable and guilty of the same offense. Their collective penalty is a prime example of

---

[13] *The Hirsch Chumash*, p. 94

Middah K'neged Middah or "measure for measure." Some might say this means the punishment fits the crime. To focus on the negative aspect of the disciplinary action in this account does injustice to the Creator. Really, *correction* might be a more effective word. G-d provides the cure for our spiritual maladies in proper doses. The Creator designed the world as a place where we could learn from errors and elevate our souls. In other words, the Creator gave us Free Will but also allows consequences to ensue. If we overcome them, we mature emotionally and spiritually in the process. If we fail to correct our behavior, then we continue in our error. Sadly, humanity has had a more tragic response by writing off negative experiences as no more than cause and effect.

Adam and Eve violated God's command by eating, therefore what followed related directly to the act of eating. Instead of their idyllic existence in *Gan Eden*, they experienced genuine hunger and were forced to labor to fill their stomachs as well as their souls.

In their new covering of skin, they had literally become consumers to survive.

Cunning words beguiled Adam and Eve, leading them away from the path of an everlasting paradise. Speech – the very instrument that separates us from the animal realm – is also the mechanism that can lead us away from G-d.

For his role, the *naHash* also ate – dust. Further, HaShem[14] declared that there would be hatred between the *naHash* and the woman. There would be strikes to its head and it would bite the '*akev* (heel) of the woman. We find in these words, the prophetic elements that point to a future rectification of '*akev*, a reference to Jacob (his name is

[14] Literally, "the Name" in Hebrew, used as a respectful reference to the *Tetragrammaton*, the four-letter name of G-d, not to be written or pronounced.

derived from the word for "heel") and a hint of his own mother's role in correcting the error of Eve.

Rabbinic commentaries often tell us that if our primal parents had not sinned, mankind would have advanced to *Olam HaBah* (World to Come). Adam and Eve had failed their first test and it was now necessary for mankind to gain crucial experience – to mature to the level where we could handle something as exquisite as *Olam Ha Bah*. Genesis 3:21 describes the Creator mercifully providing Adam and Eve with protection in the form of garments of skin prior to sending them out into the harsh physical world.

The Creator apportioned abundant blessings – both spiritual and material – to Adam, who then divided these gifts between his two sons. The tangible blessing is obviously the massive real estate of the earth. The spiritual inheritance included certain rights, such as leadership in the form of priesthood and the authority to build the future place of worship, the *Beit HaMikdash* (Holy Temple).

Cain ignored the spiritual rewards and coveted only the material blessings. This was reflected in his name, which comes from the Hebrew *kanah*, meaning to gain or acquire.[15] It was this very trait that was the catalyst for the Torah's first recorded killing of a human being by another.

Since Cain was the firstborn, Adam taught him the ritual of bringing *korban*, an offering that was placed on a *mizbeaH* or altar. There are a number of opinions as to when this occurred. One commentary teaches that Cain brought the offering at *Rosh Hashanah*. Another opinion holds that it was at the time of the year when Passover would be celebrated and that Adam instructed his firstborn to keep this prophecy

[15] It is very likely that our English word "gain" is derived from Cain.

alive by marking it with an offering.[16]

At this point, I wish to interject some thoughts regarding the ritual of sacrifice or *korban* – one of the most misunderstood and maligned practices found in the Torah. The modern reader, who believes that burnt offerings represent a backward ritual, is misjudging its place in G-d's plan.

The *korban* is vital to understanding the entire post-Garden experience and, more importantly, our personal role in the scheme of things.

Korban is more accurately rendered as "offering" and comes from *k'rav*, "to draw near." That means that its function was to bring the person making the offering closer to the Creator. This ritual, bereft of any clarification, conjures up all manner of negative imagery and hints of brutality being committed on helpless animals. However, *korban* as codified in Levitical law, is humane due to the precise manner in which the creature is slaughtered. A painful death actually defiles the offering. This is another instance in which the Torah taught, thousands of years ago, to act in a thoughtful and careful manner.

The *korban* is no more savage than the contemporary meat processing that makes an animal fit for human consumption. In fact, government-regulated slaughterhouse techniques fall short of actual *kosher* practice as mandated in the Torah. Most of the sacrifices were enjoyed in a kind of holy cookout. On the altar, the meat was roasted and became a

---

[16] *Pirke de Rabbi Rabbi Eliezer*, trans. by Gerald Friedlander (Sepher-Hermon Press, NY / 1981) p. 153

flavorful meal shared between the priests and the poor.[17] Certain offerings were not flesh, but a mixture of flour and oil. In addition, salt was always added to the offerings. Thus, the animal, vegetable and mineral realm was blessed through the ritual of *korban*.

This *mitzvah*, like all commandments in the Torah, embodied deep and meaningful teachings. One profound lesson contained in this practice is that the physical universe is sustained via a process that is literally a series of sacrifices wherein matter is continually altered from one form into another. The earth "sacrifices" minerals to plant life. The latter is kept alive because they absorb minerals. They then sustain the animal realm. This cycle of life utilizes the basic components of our material world: mineral, vegetable and animal. As we have seen, these three are also part of the *korban*.

But this operation attains a higher purpose when these same components from the animal, vegetable and mineral world are passed on to humankind. The reader will also note that this process takes place in the same basic order in which these forms of matter were created. But this sequence is marvelously elevated. We continue the process – not by dying – but by accepting the life-giving energy and offering ourselves in service to our Creator and to each other.

The ritual of *korban* is then 1) a model of how the physical realm functions, 2) how the universe is sustained, 3) of our place in the order of things and 4) our enormous responsibility to not squander this life-giving energy derived from the mineral, plant and animal world.

---

[17] Since the destruction of Israel's Holy Temple, the dinner table has served as the altar of sacrifice. In the Jewish home, the father is the priest who shares his bounty with his family and friends.

So-called animal rights groups will never understand the essential truths of the *korbanot* and shudder at the thought of killing an animal for any reason. Their efforts, bordering on the militant, are meant to equate animal life with human life – a view which could eventually lead to the acceptance of animals as sexual partners. The reader may laugh unless he has seen *Project Nim*, a documentary released in 2011. The film follows the attempts by a Columbia University researcher to prove that language was not unique to humans. He entrusted a newborn chimpanzee to a family and asked that they raise it as if it were human. Over the years, the chimp was shuttled from one home to another and the final results of the experiment are, at best inconclusive, though some experts have deemed it a failure. One of the more shocking revelations in the film comes from the woman who actually breast fed the chimp and later considered having sexual relations with the animal!

At this point, the reader is asking what has this to do with the offering of an animal. It is because the act of *korban*, replete with its many lessons, also teaches that the Creator has placed a distinct and vast division between humanity and the animal realm. The fact that G-d allows us to offer the life of an animal but never a human being speaks of this separation.

An in-depth discussion of the variety of offerings is outside the scope of this text but the reader should know that there are, basically four types of animal offerings:

The *Olah (Elevated)*

Sh'lamim (Peace offering)

Chatat (Sin offering)

Asham (Guilt offering).

The *Olah* was completely burned on the altar, except the skin of the animal, which was given to the priests. There were certain kinds of *Chatat* offerings that were burned completely, while other *Chatat korbanot* were eaten by the priests. The *Asham* were also eaten by the priests, whereas the *Sh'lamim allowed* the people to feast with the priests.

Contrary to Christian theology, the Sin Offering (C*hatat*) cannot be utilized for major transgressions of the Law. Quite the contrary, it was only for so-called minor transgressions --- committed unintentionally. This offering reminds us how easily we waste our physical and spiritual gifts through carelessness. In other words, even our thoughtlessness affects the fabric of the universe. One is allowed to exhibit gratitude by returning the animal's *nefesh* or soul to the pool of universal energy created by G-d via the Thanksgiving *korban*. In this the participant recognizes the source of all blessings.

In contrast to the misconceptions promoted by Christianity, the whole of the sacrificial system was not designed for *forgiveness* of sin – even the very first pages of Genesis disputes that idea. The offering made by Cain was brought *before* he sinned.[18]

The Thought That Counts

The whole idea of *korban* meant little to Cain. He viewed the burnt offering as a waste of good inventory. Also, his position as firstborn provoked a warped sense of entitlement. He resented giving up anything of value. The *midrash* teaches that Cain offered only a bit of flax. One can imagine him checking his stock of flax and deciding that the loss was negligible. True to his name and nature, there was

[18] To discover what the Bible actually says about the subject of sacrifices and sin, I recommend Rabbi Tovia Singer's *Let's Get Biblical* (RNBN Publishing, New York / Jerusalem, 2001)

nothing for him to *gain*. His pile of flax on the altar was rejected.

Abel made an offering culled from the best of his flocks. We know that his selection was superior to his brother's because the text describes Abel as bringing the choicest from the herds while Cain is described as simply bringing produce from the field. Rav Hirsch, in his commentary on Genesis 4:5, teaches that the Creator did not place any intrinsic value on the flax brought by Cain or even the offering from Abel's flocks. G-d looked squarely at the intent of each brother's heart.[19]

From the beginning it has always been incumbent on the one making the offering to have his head and his heart in the right place. Otherwise, it was an empty routine.

Some Christian commentators attempt to shore up the misconception that the *korbanot* have no value before G-d by quoting King David:

> You do not delight in sacrifice, or I would bring it; you do not take pleasure in burnt offerings. The sacrifices of God are a broken spirit; a broken and contrite heart, O God, you will not despise. – Psalms 51:16

However, the beginning of this particular Psalm informs us that it was written by King David. It was his response to being confronted by the prophet Nathan after David slept with Bathsheba. As the rabbinic commentator Ibn Ezra points out, David was expressing his deep realization that the offering *alone* would never atone for the complexity and serious nature of his sin.

The Creator requires that we repent or make *tshuvah* but

---

[19] *The Hirsch Chumash*, pp. 126-127

the act is completely without merit unless fueled by a purity of motivation. This idea applies to any scripture that mentions the Creator's unhappiness with an offering that is devoid of a spiritual component. David understood that he could never begin to approach the altar unless he had a broken spirit and contrite heart *in tandem* with his offering. What we do in the physical world does impact the spiritual realm. Though the Creator knows our hearts, He desires that we make the effort to recognize what is really in our hearts. Proper *korbanot* or offerings are infused with an understanding of one's role in the act.

Whole chapters of Torah are replete with specific directives from G-d on the proper method of performing offerings. When we dismiss these instructions with the charge that they have no meaning for us today, we trivialize the commands of G-d and turn His words into idle chatter. Sadly, it is a basic tenet of Christianity to diminish the true role of *korbanot* and characterize this aspect of Jewish belief as outmoded. At the same time, they advance the wrong-headed conceit that Jesus' death replaced the sacrifices once and for all. The very words of the prophets vividly *contradict* this notion and promise a time when offerings will be very much a part of our worship in the Temple:

> And foreigners who bind themselves to HaShem to serve him and to love the name of HaShem to become servants to Him, all who guard the Sabbath against desecration, and grasp my covenant tightly — I bring them to My holy mountain and will gladden them in My house of prayer; **Their elevation offerings and feast offerings will find favor on My Altar, for My House will be called a house of prayer for all the peoples.**
>
> — Isaiah 56: 6-7

> For thus said HaShem: "There should never be cut off from David a man who sits on the throne of the House of Israel. And for the Kohanim, the Levites, there will **never be cut off a man from before me who offers elevation-offerings and burns meal offerings and performs feast offerings all the days.**"[20]
>
> — Jeremiah 33: 17-18

Ultimately, anyone who diminishes the value of the sacrificial system and labels it invalid, reveals that they are heirs of the philosophy of Cain, Esau and every other Biblical figure who rejected the words of the Creator.

[20] Text bolded by the author for emphasis

Chapter Four

READY TO RUMBLE

Cain was unhappy about a series of imagined abuses when Abel brought his *korban*. It was the last straw.

Adam had given his sons equal portions to possess. But Cain believed he should have received a double inheritance since he was the eldest.

In an attempt to pacify his older brother, Abel agreed that Cain retained all lands while Abel kept the rights to all movable property. When Cain discovered Abel's sheep grazing on his land, he cried foul and declared a breach of their agreement.[21] Cain insisted that the sheep be removed from his land – which was impossible since all the land was owned by Cain. Abel countered with a demand that Cain return the clothes he was wearing since the garments were a by-product of Abel's livestock.

Another point of contention was that each of them believed that they alone would possess the site of the future *Beit HaMikdash* (Holy Temple).

Cain also coveted the beautiful wife of Abel.

When Cain discovered Abel alone in the field one day, they began to argue about some of these very issues. The Torah relates that Cain "rose up" to kill his brother. This description is used because the quarrel escalated into a violent wrestling match and it was actually Abel who got the upper hand. Cain, pinned beneath his brother, pleaded to be released. Abel, moved by compassion, let him go. Cain, still seething with wild rage, jumped to his feet and killed his

---

[21] In other words, Cain owned *all* real estate.

unsuspecting brother.[22]

History has been witness to the same scenario throughout the centuries – the Jewish people would show kindness to their mortal enemies who would then turn on them with devastating consequences. In the days of Esther, the attempted annihilation of her people in Persia was the result of Esther's ancestor, King Saul, showing leniency to his enemy Agag. The Amalekite king lived long enough to conceive the ancestor of Haman, who attempted to wipe out every Jew in the Persian Empire. No wonder the sages teach, "He who is compassionate to the cruel will ultimately be cruel to the compassionate."

Nations and clans would invoke Cain's grievances which stem from arrogance and greed. Recall how Cain's name speaks of a totally acquisitive persona. His soul, permeated with materialism, wanted to possess everything in his reach. On the other hand, Abel (Hevel), whose name meant vapor or vanity, understood that everything came from the invisible G-d but that material possessions would eventually vanish. Abel was continually grateful for whatever he was given because he recognized the Creator as his source of life and its gifts.

Though Abel perished, the commentary known as *Da'ath Zekenim* cites G-d's acceptance of his offering, just before his death, as proof that he would merit to live in the Next World.[23]

---

[22] Rabbi Yaakov Culi, *The Torah Anthology, (MeAm Lo'ez*) Book One, translated by Rabbi Aryeh Kaplan (Moznaim Publishing Corporation NY/ Jerusalem 1989), pp. 288-281

[23] Genesis 4:4 /Commentary by Rabbi A.J. Rosenberg (Book of Genesis/ Vol 1 /Judaica Press/NY/1993) p. 65

Cain was given two chances to turn his life around. At first, G-d asked Cain if he knew where his brother was. Why would the Creator of the universe need to ask such a question? As with everything in the Torah, the question is there to teach us something. It demonstrates that G-d gives us the benefit of the doubt and thus, we should do the same for each other. The question remains with us even though Cain shrugged it off with the well-known response, “Am I my brother’s keeper?” From that very day forward, the Creator repeatedly inquires if we are concerned for our brother.

The first killing in history is what contemporary courts would call a crime of passion. It was not premeditated. Technically, it was manslaughter. Cain, blinded by anger, didn’t consider that his actions would result in the death of his brother. His sentence is the precedent for the Torah ruling that allowed a person convicted of manslaughter to be remanded to a kind of house arrest known in the Torah as a City of Refuge.[24]

G-d judged Cain based on these facts and allowed him to live. The Creator even attempted to rehabilitate Cain by teaching him that he could be a better man, that his passions were actually a powerful engine that he could harness to rectify his error. The destiny of Cain was sealed when he rejected this loving instruction. He continued to ignore the existential lesson of the *korban* – that the Creator wants us to elevate our lives by offering ourselves in service to our brothers.

Though all the earth belonged to him, Cain wandered from one region to another raising families and building cities to house them. He was a global land developer motivated not by altruism but the desire to protect and sustain what he believed was his by birthright. Most of humankind followed in the footsteps of Cain. A world, schooled on material

[24] Numbers 35:22

possession was a place fed by a desire to own everything. It was a way of life that degenerated into a world of robbery and violence. Sexual depravity, another symptom, was so pervasive that it contaminated animal life and polluted the soil. There were innocent people but they were in constant danger of being wiped out by those trafficking in violence. The world was on the brink of total destruction.

G-d brought the Flood to save the planet.

A New World

The global disaster we call The Flood is known, in Hebrew, as the *Mabbul*. According to Rashi, the esteemed Medieval Torah commentator, this unique word actually means "exhaustion" or "to wither away" and indicates how the flood waters depleted the ground of its substantial mineral content.[25] Other commentaries reveal that super-heated hydrothermal "fountains of the deep" burst forth and leached away the powerful, enriched nutrients from the soil. The entire food chain was affected so severely that it contributed to the diminished life spans of the post-Flood generations. The *Talmud* teaches that the *Mabbul* occurred in two stages. Initially, only one-third of the earth was flooded but when humanity failed to change, a global catastrophe ensued. Before that happened, Noah was instructed to build a *tevah* or ark.

Most of us are familiar with the Gilgamesh Epic, said to be a forerunner of the flood story in Genesis. However, there is an ancient text that predates it by centuries and is found on the Atrahasis tablets. The latter also offers the tale of an epic Flood.

The tale, inscribed in Akkadian, unfolds as the character

---

[25] Rashi is an acronym for Rabbi Shlomo Yitzhaki (1040 - 1105)

called Atrahasis is given a seven-day warning of the approaching flood. In Genesis, Noah and his sons enter the ark seven days before the *Mabbul*. They knew it was time because Noah's grandfather, Methuselah, had just died. The reader will recall that names of Torah figures are prophetic and this was true of Methuselah whose name roughly translates to "his death sends destruction." The sages relate that Noah and his family entered the ark and sat *shiva*, the seven-day mourning period– then the rains came.[26]

After spending a year in the ark, Noah, with his sons Ham, Shem, Japheth, and their wives, departed from the ark and built an altar. He did so with the intent of bringing *korban* in the form of a thanksgiving offering. This was one of the reasons why Noah was instructed to preserve seven pairs of clean animals, along with pairs of unclean animals. Bible skeptics are often confused by the two separate verses dealing with the command by G-d to bring animals into the ark. If one ignores the original meaning found in the Hebrew text, the verses seem to appear contradictory. What is often misunderstood is that the first command, in Genesis 6:19-20, is a *minimum requirement* and instructs Noah to select only males and females that met two criteria: 1) the animal was to be a distinct, pure form of the species and 2) uncorrupted. Those requirements were necessary due to bizarre crossbreeding, as well as rampant bestiality in the era of the Flood. The next command, found in Genesis 7:2-4, is even more specific and adds an additional provision that Noah must choose *mikol habehemah hatehorah* ("from all clean animals"), meaning he was to choose out pairs of seven from among those animals meeting the first set of criteria. These creatures were to be collected in pairs of seven to insure there would be an abundance of the species dedicated as kosher for consumption and, later as offerings for Israel. The Creator was also insuring clean animals would

[26] *Bereshith Rabba* on the *parsha Noah* in Genesis 7:4

also be available for Noahides for use in their offerings. Rabbi Samson Raphael Hirsch further explains:

> This means that even in those early days, man was required to make this distinction – namely in connection with offerings. For Noahides were permitted and are permitted to offer only pure animals (Zevachim 115b). Thus, Jews are permitted to eat only those animals that are fit to be offered by all men. The table of Israel and the altar of the Noahides stand on the same level.[27]

Note that Rav Hirsch, in the last statement, underscores the idea that eating kosher animals is a strictly Jewish commandment while Noahides are only required to use kosher animals for *korbanot*. Non-Jews are not commanded to consume kosher food. That said, some suggest that because a Noahide cannot be sure if slaughtering practices are always humane, one should eat kosher meats. I should stress that there is no consensus on this issue, at this writing.

The post-Flood offering and its acceptance by the Creator marked the beginning of a permanent covenant with Noah and his descendants. In such agreements, both parties consent to certain terms. Among the promises made to Noah, G-d established four seasons for the growth and harvesting of crops. The Creator also pledged never to cover the earth completely with water. In effect, G-d reset an orderly system to always function – even flourish and provide a home for humanity.

---

[27] *The Hirsch Chumash, Sefer Bereshis*, p. 189

The Seven Laws of Noah

Noah pledged to keep laws that were originally given to Adam. Six of them were in place prior to the *Mabbul*. There was a seventh additional decree instituted so that post-Flood humanity could derive nourishment from animal life but with a provision against cruelty by forbidding the consumption of the flesh taken from a living creature. Theses seven precepts are known as the *Sheva Mitzvoth B'nei Noah*, aka the Seven Laws of Noah, the Noahide Laws, Seven Universal Laws and other designations. Though they are not specifically stated in the Written Torah, they come to us via the Oral Torah.

According to the Rambam, in his *Mishne Torah*, the Seven Laws were repeated to Moses on Mount Sinai along with the 613 laws given to the nation of Israel. The sages teach that the first six laws are embedded in Genesis 2:16, where it is stated that, 'the Lord commanded Adam..." In the ninth chapter of Genesis, when Noah departed from the ark, all seven precepts can be derived from the words of the Creator, as well as the new directive:

Do Not Eat the Limb of a Living Animal

> But flesh; with its soul, its blood you shall not eat.
>
> – Genesis 9:4

This actual rendering, from the Hebrew is meant to express a prohibition against eating flesh "with the life still in it."

The other six commandments are derived from the words spoke to Noah by the Creator.

Do Not Murder

> But of man, every man for that of his brother I will demand the soul of man. Whoever sheds the blood of man, by man shall his blood be shed;
>
> – Genesis 9:5-6

This includes a prohibition against suicide and murder. These words also contain the source of another Noahide commandment...

Do Establish Courts of Justice

> Whoever sheds the blood of man, by man shall his blood be shed;
>
> – Genesis 9:6

The operative phrase is, "by man shall his blood be shed," which places full responsibility on humanity to bring a murderer to justice. The Creator established the necessity for capital punishment. He would not allow the post-Flood generation to fall into the folly of thinking, as the antediluvians had, that a killer who remains alive does so because G-d, somehow accepted his murderous act.

Do Not Commit Idolatry

It is understood, in the context of G-d's command to Noah, that we keep the Seven Laws because the Creator requires us to do so. Observing them only because we deem them logical is to elevate our thoughts above G-d, in essence, we are worshipping our own ideas. We are the idol.

Do Not Blaspheme G-d

Rejecting the Creator and His words is blasphemy.

Do Not Commit Sexual Immorality

Be fruitful and multiply, teem on the earth and multiply on it.

— Genesis 9: 7

We are encouraged to have children and populate the earth. Sexual immorality negates the idea of being fruitful since such acts are wholly selfish and rarely result in the creation of a child. It also impedes the concept of a family unit so vital to maintaining a just and peaceful society.

Do Not Commit Theft

The prohibition against Theft is encompassed in all of the previous laws since murder and adultery constitute very real forms of stealing. Idolatry and Blasphemy are theft since they rob the Creator of the honor and love that is rightfully His.

In Genesis 9:8, beginning with the words, *"I will establish my covenant with you,"* and concluding with, *"this is a sign of the everlasting covenant,"* the word *brit* or covenant, is found exactly seven times. This universal code serves as a template for maintaining an orderly, civilized society. Look at any culture throughout history that has ignored these guiding principles – there is rapid decline or they simply fail to advance.

When Joshua arrived at the borders of Canaan, he offered a peace treaty that included a stipulation to keep the Noahide Laws. The tribes inhabiting the land were so deeply depraved that they rejected the treaty. This explains Genesis 15:16, and how Abraham's descendants would possess the land after *"the wickedness of the Amorite was full..."*

This was another reason that Israel could not possess Canaan until they had spent forty years in the wilderness. They had to wait until the righteous gentiles (those who kept the Seven Laws) in Canaan had eventually passed away before the Twelve Tribes could enter. If they had agreed to keep the Seven Laws, Joshua would have allowed the Canaanites to remain under the status of a *Ger Toshav.*[28]

This status today is what we would call a resident alien. Under Torah law, if the *Ger Toshav* desires, he or she can take on the status of a *Ger Tzedek* which is not unlike the modern designation of the naturalized citizen. Under the present system, we know this as conversion. We will see this distinction revert to its true meaning when Israel becomes a wholly and holy Torah government. In reality, the *Ger Tzedek* is not joining a religion but a nation.

---

[28] *Hilchot Melakihim* (Laws of the Kings) 6:10 in the *Mishne Torah*

Losing My Religion

Mainstream theology ignores or is unaware of the Seven Laws of Noah. They commit a major error by insisting that Jew and non-Jew alike are subject to the first Ten Commandments found in Exodus 20:1-14. However, those commandments are only the first ten of an entire body of laws, totaling 613. They are designed for the nation of Israel so that the Jews can function in their own land and with each other as a holy people. At Sinai, G-d gave the entire Torah to those standing there and clarified exactly who He was addressing with this very simple preamble:

> I am the Lord, thy G-d who has taken you out of the land of Egypt, out of the house of bondage.
>
> – Exodus 20:2

There is no ambiguity in these words. The Creator is speaking to a specific people whose existence and purpose remains unique in all history. More to the point, G-d is addressing a nation – not a religion:

> I will make you into a great nation. I will bless you and make you great. You shall become a blessing.
>
> – Genesis 12:2

Abraham was never promised that he would become a great religion. He was promised nationhood and it was actualized when G-d took the Twelve Tribes out of Egypt and led them to a mountain located in a desolate patch of ground that no kingdom claimed:

> You will be a kingdom of priests and a holy nation to Me.
>
> – Exodus 19:6

Consider how often Judaism is referenced as one of, "the

world's three great religions" and how the words – unchallenged – promote a kind of relativism that allows true observance of Torah to be lumped into the same category as Christianity and Islam. Western thought promotes the philosophy that there must be a clear disconnect between belief in the Creator and government for any nation to function. In reality, a genuine Torah government would never separate belief and law or faith and everyday life.

Stating that one is a Jew should carry the same meaning as saying that one is American, Japanese or any nationality. In fact, when a person *converts* (an unfortunate term) to Judaism, they become a naturalized citizen of a great and ancient commonwealth still thriving today. The convert is subject to all of the laws of that commonwealth. Just as the children born to a naturalized citizen are automatically considered citizens of their parent's adopted nation, children born to *converts* are considered Jewish. Obviously, there are certain things a convert cannot do but, again, there are similar statutes in the U. S. Constitution. Just as a naturalized American citizen cannot hold certain public offices, there are restrictions that limit those who can be *Kohanim*, as well as certain leadership positions firmly established by G-d with the Twelve Tribes and their attendant rights under Torah Law. For example, the kingship is reserved for the tribe of Judah.

A Jew can make the same claim as any nation: in their Torah they possess a set of laws covering every aspect of daily life and they have a land in which to practice those laws. However, there is one elegant and amazing difference: Any law that I observe, for example, obeying a traffic sign, only maintains order. But when a Jew keeps any Torah command, even one that might be viewed as the simplest *mitzvah*--- that Jew brings down holiness into the world! Israel is unique in this way and also by virtue of the fact that they are the only nation in history that was created by G-d.

> So said the Lord, Who gives the sun to illuminate by day, the laws of the moon and the stars to illuminate at night, Who stirs up the sea and its waves roar, the Lord of Hosts is His name. If these laws depart from before Me, says the Lord, so will the seed of Israel cease being a nation before Me for all time.
>
> – Jeremiah 31:34-35

What a marvelous thing this is. This idea of nationhood is so elementary, so basic, that it can be seen in the even worst English translations of the Tanakh. I would also add that being Jew has little to do with skin color and there are a myriad of flesh tones and bloodlines that make up this holy nation.

If the world could grasp this one fundamental truth – that the people called Israel are *not an ethnic group, not a religion but rather a nation made up of many ethnic groups who worship the One true G-d* – then the role and mission of the Jews would be understood. The Torah was given to both instruct Israel and to sanction explicit laws for every facet of their life as a nation. If fervent and well-meaning evangelicals would understand that the Torah was given only to the Jewish people to serve, on one level, as the original Constitution of Israel, then those same evangelicals would realize any attempt to convert Jews is tantamount to violating the sovereignty of Israel. I will even be so bold as to state that trying to convert a Jew is asking them to commit treason.

Clearly, there must come a day when, the modern State of

Israel will grasp the concept of true Jewish nationhood. It may only happen only when every Jewish family in the *galuth* boards a plane for the land that the Creator gave them. Most importantly, a genuine Jewish nation will only emerge when the Jews living in eretz Israel demand a Torah government. The creation of Israel represented a unique partnership in which G-d provides the necessities crucial for a life of sacrifice to G-d and humanity.

Perhaps we should relegate the usage of the word "religion" to that of an adjective. Certainly Israel, as envisioned in the Torah, is a religious nation; the Jews can be characterized as living religious lives. Even Noahides, sometimes called Righteous Gentiles, should be religious in their daily conduct. The problem is one of semantics, especially when we consider the fact that there is no word in Hebrew for religion.

It may come as a shock to the reader, but faithfully observing the Seven Laws of Noah is also not a religion – even though the first two commandments are against Idolatry and Blasphemy. Yes, we are to believe in our Creator. It is a religious way of life but not a religion. A more accurate expression is "ethical monotheism".

As Vendyl Jones, of blessed memory, was fond of saying, "Religion gets in the way of my faith in G-d."

At this point, I will defer to Torah scholar and good friend, Rabbi Michael Shelomo Bar-Ron, who sums up the matter concisely and eloquently in his *Guide For the Noahide*:

> The Noahide Covenant is not a religion that one must convert to, a people one must be accepted into. It is the Divinely-ordained

> legal, social, moral, and spiritual framework of physical laws and limitations.....
>
> *Beyond the legal definition, it is a birthright – a free gift to anyone born into this world – as the basic moral foundation for a life in harmony with the creator and other people.*[29]

I can only add that this is the ultimate purpose for humanity as seen in the Torah --- a world that functions not as a set of vast and disparate ideologies --- but as a planet of nations whose belief in the Creator is the core of our purpose and existence.

The great Jewish sage Maimonides, better known as the Rambam,[30] explains and illuminates the Seven Laws of Noah in his monumental *Mishne Torah*, in the section, *Hilchot Melakhim*. He also states that it is incumbent on the Jewish People to teach the nations of the world these laws. These universal precepts are not new. Nor are they, as the less-informed would have us believe, a devious plot to enslave the non-Jewish world. Great minds such as Sir Isaac Newton embraced the concept of the Noahide Laws and expounded on them in his day. Newton was fascinated by the study of Torah and found that it complemented his abiding interest in science. He was especially intrigued by the study of the *Mishkan* (the Tabernacle), as well as the Temple.

---

[29] See Rabbi Bar-Ron's *Guide for the Noahide* (Lightcatcher Books, Springdale, Ar, 2010) p. 3

[30] An acronym for Rabbi Moses Ben Maimon

Some have thought that Newton was a secret Jew, but a recent discovery of his papers reveals a genius who, though he was called a Christian, was very much at odds with the beliefs of the Church in his day. He respected and admired the teachings of Torah and *Talmud*.[31] Like many other Hebraists of his time, such as the Dutch jurist Hugo Grotius, he cited the Noahide Laws as the source for establishing international law. There was John Selden, who drew inspiration and direction from the Torah. These men understood the importance of the Seven Laws and used them to forge landmark concepts for justice and the rule of law.[32] John Selden broke new legal ground in his day with the publication of an expansive study of the Torah jurisprudence, the Sanhedrin and the Seven Laws known by its abbreviated title as *De Synedriis*.

For the reader who wishes to explore the subject of the Noahide Laws there are a number of relevant sources.[33]

Had the Creator required the entire world to come under all 613 commandments in the Torah, He would have presented that body of Divine direction to all of humankind. However, He *chose* Israel, a people who specifically experienced the Egyptian exile in preparation for acceptance of the Torah at Sinai. Hence, they are called the Chosen People — not because they deserved it — but because they possessed the potential to take on the role of a nation of priests. Their very DNA carried the noble traits of their ancestor Abraham. In upcoming chapters we will look at the life of this

---

[31] Article by Rabbi Eliezer Isaacovitz, "*The Last Secrets of Sir Isaac Newton*" (Mishpacha Magazine, September 2009)pp. 26-31

[32] Paul Eidelberg, *Toward a Renaissance of Israel and America* (Lightcatcher Books, Springdale, AR, 2009) p. 27

[33] See the Bibliography for books and resources at the conclusion of the book.

remarkable patriarch.

Noah faced the monumental task of building a new world into a place of peace and prosperity for all of humanity. But one of his sons chose to ignore the Seven Laws and disrupted those plans.

Noah exited the ark and planted a vineyard. The real trouble began with the production of wine. Noah probably needed a stiff drink considering how he had survived a global disaster and was faced with rebuilding the world. He imbibed to excess and became amorous with his wife.

The *Midrash* reveals that Canaan, the son of Ham, saw Noah uncovered and reported this to his father. Ham became alarmed at the prospect of another brother. That meant another heir which would deprive Ham of an even larger share of the earth's lands. The opinions of the sages differ. Some say it was Canaan while others hold that Ham went into Noah's tent and castrated him. Shocked and humiliated Noah cried:

> Cursed is Canaan; a slave of slaves shall he be to his brothers.
>
> — Genesis 9:25

You will note that his reference was to Canaan, instead of Ham. The fact that Canaan was the object of Noah's wrath may be the clue that it was actually Canaan who initiated the tragic episode. Additional reasons are cited. Since Ham "cursed" Noah, making him unable to have a son, Noah cursed the son of Ham. Another explanation for cursing Canaan was because G-d had already blessed Ham, thus he could not be cursed.[34]

[34] Genesis 9:1

The modern reader tends to regard Noah's words as some kind of dark enchantment or spell. But Noah was expressing prophetic insight infused with a deeply heartbreaking realization. He could see that Canaan was already under the corrupt influence of Ham and that it was so pervasive that Canaan's progeny were doomed to be schooled in Ham's self-centered and cruel ways.

Canaan, like his father, was already a slave to his material needs and ensnared by his passions.[35] Therefore, he instilled in his offspring, a mentality that could readily accept slavery out of a need to sustain those passions. Noah was struck by the truth that the apple did not fall far from the tree. At that moment, he saw the new world would be filled again with rotten apples.

---

[35] Canaan is derived from *kana*, which is to subdue or degrade.

Chapter Five

TEMPLATE FOR TYRANNY

A politician is one that would circumvent God.
— Shakespeare[36]

The descendants of Noah thrived and traveled from the mountains of Ararat to settle in a plain called *Shinar*. It would seem that they might rebuild the world anew, under the divine direction of a loving G-d. However, the figure that we know as Nimrod decided that his policies were better.

You will recall that after Adam and Eve were expelled from *Gan Eden*, G-d clothed them in animal skins. Though the Torah is alluding to a significant change that affected their very being, it also implies actual garments. They were quite remarkable and considered to be royal finery in the manner of priestly robes. The righteous lineage of Adam was to inherit them. They were passed down to Seth and eventually to Noah. When he boarded the ark, Noah kept these robes among his treasures. Ham stole the garments worn by Adam, gave them to Cush, who then bestowed them on his son Nimrod. As noted in the previous chapter, Ham was a corrupt patriarch whose tainted influence had already spread to his offspring. It was Cush who repeated the transgression of robbery that had hastened the devastation of the antediluvian world. It was this theft that launched Nimrod's career and provided impetus for his ascent to power. While clad in this remarkable clothing, he believed that he was

[36] A popular, though heavily paraphrased quote that comes from *Hamlet*, Act 5, Scene 10: "That skull had a tongue in it and could sing once. How the knave jowls it to the ground, as if it were Cain's jawbone, that did the first murder! It might be the pate of a politician, which this ass now o'erreaches, one that would circumvent God, might it not?"

invulnerable to any attack, especially from animals.[37] As we shall see, in another chapter, this prized garment figures significantly in another Biblical event.

In the tenth chapter of Genesis Nimrod is listed separately from the other sons of Cush:

> He began to be powerful in the earth. He was a
>
> mighty trapper before G-d. It is therefore said,
>
> "Like Nimrod, a mighty hunter before G-d."
>
> – Genesis 10:8-9

The placement of Nimrod's name apart from his siblings in the text is an allusion to the cultic worship that arose around him. Nimrod came to prominence as a world-class hunter and was literally idolized by the masses. He may have even been the inspiration of ancient champions such as Hercules. Some classical secular sources even mention that he was a giant.[38]

Rashi relates that the description of Nimrod as a "trapper" is a reference to his extraordinary talents as an astute and charismatic politician. The Torah underscores that persona by describing him as carrying out his actions *before G-d* – literally, an affront to the Creator. The name, Nimrod, comes from *marod*, to rebel. Our English word, "marauder," is derived from this same Hebrew root.

Nimrod actively promoted the illusion that he had divine origins. Just as he clad himself in the priestly robes of Adam, he clothed his lust for power in false piety. The effect was

---

[37] *The Torah Anthology (MeAm Lo'ez)* Book One pp. 404-405

[38] *The Works of Philo of Alexandria*, trans. by C.D. Yonge (Hendrickson Publishers, Inc, 1993) p. 840

that the people surrendered their own liberties. And because he was not content with only ruling over the beasts, Nimrod was the first to inaugurate wars and the concept of kingship after the Flood. Under his leadership, the people united to build the infamous Tower of Babel.

Towering Egos

Pardon the pun, but the Tower of Babel represented a major landmark for humankind. Through brute strength and military prowess, Nimrod mobilized the masses in a tower project. They believed, like him, that human intellect combined with physical force could shape the world. Mesmerized by his charisma, they joined him in a united effort:

> The whole earth was of one language and a common purpose.
>
> — Genesis 11:1

It is significant that the Hebrew word *lashon*, meaning tongue or language, is not found in the above verse. Instead, it reads *saphah*, a word that carries the connotation of completion and limitation. The Torah teaches that G-d loves unity, so seeing the people were of one accord was not problematic for the Creator — it was the fact that their designs rejected His instruction. The Oral Tradition relates that there were three camps — each with different agendas — but unified to build a great city and the Tower.

This unholy trinity espoused beliefs in varying degrees, from religious to outright atheism. One group, representing the religious faction, built the tower so that it would "reach to the heavens." They may have even believed that they were doing the work of G-d. But it was *their image* of Him. They saw a Being who could never judge or execute judgment — certainly nothing like a global flood. Their favorite phrase was likely, "My god would never kill anyone." It was in the heights of this edifice that they planned to build a place of worship to a deity who represented their own values.

The politicians led the next camp. They said, "let us make a name for ourselves," and fostered a so-called progressive ideology. They viewed, with contempt, anyone who believed in an invisible Creator and accused the faithful of slowing mankind from moving forward. The Tower politicos wanted to jettison what they considered pre-Flood, old-world thinking. The tower allowed them military superiority by literally holding the highest ground. This illusion was buttressed by their boast that they would storm heaven and make war on the Creator. This could be achieved by subjugating and, if need be, annihilating anyone who believed in Him.

The third group comprised the scientific community whose aim was to prevent being, "scattered abroad over the face of the earth." It was their contention that since the Flood occurred 1,656 years from the birth of Adam that it was surely a cyclical event. The tower would serve as protection from another catastrophe when the planets aligned once again in the same configuration when 1,656 years had passed.

The common character trait that bound the masses at the Tower was embodied in the very essence of *saphah*. They were convinced of their own completeness; they required nothing further than their own knowledge and armed might to achieve a better world. Paradoxically, by espousing this view, their vision was tragically limited because they rejected the supernal instruction, wisdom and guidance of G-d. The ideologies that drove the tower builders can be traced back to the fatalistic world-view of Cain, who limited his philosophy to the physical senses and worship of the sensual. His humanistic outlook had survived the Flood through Ham, Canaan, Cush and was advanced by Nimrod.

Noah had seen the direction that Canaan had taken and prophesied that a man, no better than a slave, could control the destiny of his descendants. Nimrod surely was enslaved, not only to physical pleasures but also his raging egotism and love of gain. Rabbi Samson Raphael Hirsch, commenting on a similar but later episode in the Torah, explains how a people allow tyrants to rule them:

> There are nations that avoid thinking for themselves and unload their concerns onto the head of a king. This occurs particularly in nations where the citizens are busily preoccupied with themselves. People who pursue comfort and wealth and ignore the idealistic interests of their community are ready to sacrifice rights and assets – so long as they are "excused from thinking."[39]

As King Solomon wrote in *Kohelet* (Ecclesiastes), there is nothing new under the sun; Nimrod and those who welcomed his autocratic rule were the original Socialists. Thankfully, there were individuals who rejected Nimrod's schemes. One such figure was Asshur, son of Shem and founder of the Assyrian Empire. As he witnessed the tower taking shape, he knew it was time to pull up stakes.

> Out of the land went forth Asshur and he built
>
> Nineveh, Rehoboth, Ir, Calah and Resen.
>
> – Genesis 10:11-12

[39] *The Hirsch Chumash, Sefer Bereshis*, p. 324

Monumental Confusion

Nimrod's realm is outlined in Genesis 10:10. Included in the list of the city-states he founded is Acadia. The latter is obviously the region historians now call Akkad, which grew out of Sumer. The archaeological record seems to confirm that the inhabitants of post-Flood Shinar and the Sumerian culture are the same people. Their innovations are very much like that of a people forced to rebuild civilization after a catastrophe.

The kingdom of Nimrod encompassed much of the Fertile Crescent, but his seat of power began in *Shinar* or Sumer. The Sumerians are said to have invented writing, wheeled devices and kiln-fired bricks. The latter process is straight from the Biblical account of the Tower of Babel. The sages tell us that the Shinar plain lacked the kind of stone required for their ambitious project. Brick making was a necessary method for erecting buildings without quarrying rock: "...and the bricks served them as stone."

While Iraq could very well be the Biblical Erech, it is confirmed by archaeological finds that it is also the location of the *later* Babylonian Empire, during the time of Nebuchadnezzar. As to the earlier realm of Nimrod, there are clues that argue in favor of Southeast Turkey as the first seat of power established by Nimrod. His domain was expansive and according to the Torah, he established several cities:

> The beginning of his kingdom was Babel, Erech, Accad, and Calneh in the land of Shinar.
>
> – Genesis 10: 10

There is a tendency to place Shinar as one separate region in present-day Iraq. But the phrase "land of Shinar" is clearly a geographical designation for Nimrod's entire domain and all of its protectorates.

To view the phrase in a modern context, we all know that America began as thirteen colonies on the eastern seaboard and eventually spread to the Pacific coast. Even though Los Angeles is on the opposite end of the continent from the original colonial states, it is obviously considered part of America. So the sense of the verse cited above from Genesis 10:10 would indicate that Babel, Erech, Accad and Calneh could be a kind of United States of Shinar.

Nimrod could have planted his banner in Southeastern Turkey eventually extending his rule toward the South and East to present-day Iraq. The Torah tells us that, after the ark of Noah landed on the mountains of Ararat:

> ...it came to pass, when they migrated from the east they found a valley in the land of Shinar and settled there.
>
> – Genesis 11:2

Note that Noah's descendants traveled *from* the east.

Consult a map and trace a line from Mount Ararat to Iraq and you will quickly see that if one journeys from the mountains of Ararat down to Iraq, one is moving south and deeper *into the east* – not away from it. This migration pattern of Noah's descendants clearly contradicts the idea that they beat a path to Iraq. Modern travelers in Turkey have noted that rugged terrain around Ararat makes a southwesterly route the most natural corridor away from the mountain.

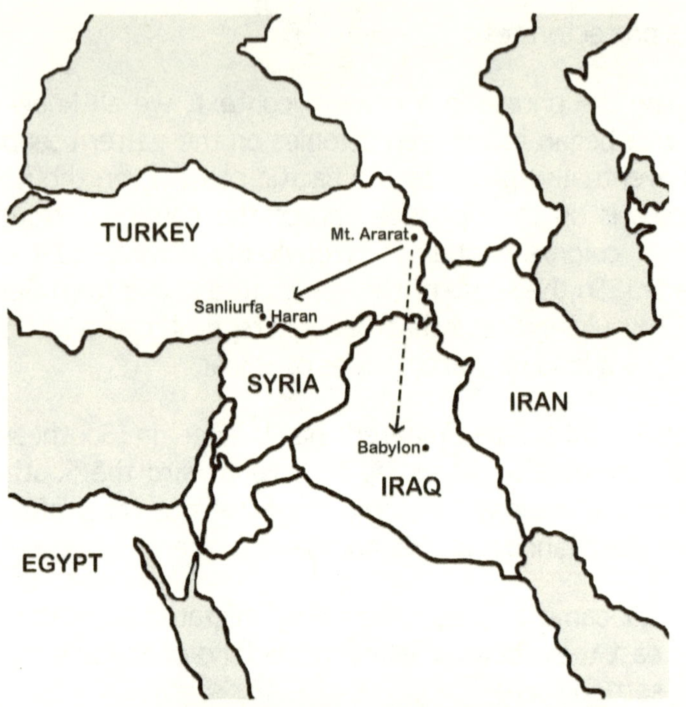

- - - - - - - Generally accepted Route of Noah's Descendants
------ Proposed Route based on Genesis 11:2

There are other geographic clues. Haran, Turkey, just south of Sanliurfa, is associated with the brother of Abraham. If one travels a few miles East of the same city is a district, in the Diyarbakır Province called Cinar (pronounced "shee-nash"). Only a few miles Southwest is Suruc, a town once known as Serugh, which recalls the great-grandfather of Abraham. To the east of Sanliurfa is Mardin, a name found in the story of Nimrod – it was his son, Mardon.

Finally, is it possible that the origin for the name of the country Turkey is derived from the father of Abraham? The Oral Tradition teaches that Terah was a high ranking official:

> And Terah the son of Nahor, the prince of Nimrod's host, was in those days very great in the

> sight of the king and his subjects, and the king and his princes loved him, and they elevated him very high.
>
> – *Sefer HaYashar* 8:49

The name Terah, in Hebrew, ends with a guttural *het*, therefore pronounced *tear-akh*. With this in mind, it's interesting to note that the oldest known reference to Turkey was found on the 8th century Orkhon inscription to the ancient Turkish people as *Turuk*.

In addition to geographical details, Genesis 11:2 has an added layer of meaning for us. The departure of the people from the landing place of the ark, the vessel that had preserved humankind, symbolizes a spiritual departure from the righteous philosophy that Noah had hoped to preserve. The name of the place they founded, *Shinar*, shares the same root as *shinah*. The latter is a Hebrew word generally interpreted as year but it can also mean a cycle or a repetition. In other words, the post-Flood generation was about to repeat the mistakes of the past.

Breaking Up Is Hard To Do

> For three things the earth doth quake, and for four
>
> it cannot endure: For a servant when he reigneth...
>
> – Proverbs 30:21-22

The Tower of Babel was destined to fall for any number of reasons, but it was the hubris of the builders and their utter reliance on man-made technology that would ultimately destabilize their efforts to forge a sprawling Nimrodian empire. The task was driven by such ruthless ambition that they nearly lost their humanity. If a clumsy worker dropped a brick from the loftiest level of the tower, they would wail over the mishap. But if a laborer fell to his death, they did not stop their work to grieve the loss. Ultimately, the very earth would cease to support their project. According to *Seder Ha Olam* the tower fell in the 1,996th year from Adam. It was the same year the continents split.[40]

In the 10th chapter of Genesis, verse 8, we read that, *"Cush begot Nimrod..."* then reading down to verse 25, we learn Eber had two sons and, *"The name of the first was Peleg, for in his days the earth was divided."*

Remember, names are prophetic. The last part of this verse reveals that the year Peleg died was also when, "the earth was divided." It was the immense seismic activity that accompanied a shift in the tectonic plates that brought the structure tumbling down. The Torah tells of the aftermath of this catastrophe:

> And G-d dispersed them from there over the face

[40] Rabbi Mattis Kantor, *Codex Judaica* (Zichron Press, New York, 2005) p. 59

of the whole earth.

— Genesis 11:8

The builders of the Tower experienced a major split in every sense of the word. With their speech confounded and their plans dashed, humanity was sent packing across the globe. Here, we see Divine justice again being meted out, measure for measure. Since the Tower design was driven by three ideologies, it was broken into three sections. *Sefer HaYashar* relates that the edifice was decimated from the bottom up.

First, a massive earthquake swallowed the tower's base. A raging fire consumed the next section. The final third, the lofty summit of the tower, spilled out across the plains of Shinar. The terrible images of the imploding Twin Towers in New York spring to mind. The sight must have been much the same but on a vastly larger scale. The circumference of the ancient debris field is described as a three-day walk. The remnants may be the previously mentioned *Nemrut Dagh*, in Southeastern Turkey.

The Jewish Sages teach that, "the world stands on three pillars: Torah, Divine service and acts of kindness."[41] Had the builders found their inspiration in those principles, perhaps their monumental task might have withstood any seismic onslaught. The one third that remained may be symbolic of at least one of those principles: kindness. G-d preserved the lives of the builders, despite of their rebellion. It was to their credit that they were, at the very least, united in their task. The Creator does approve of harmony between His children. Centuries later, a structure would be built that, indeed, embodied Torah, Divine service and acts of kindness. It was *Beit HaMikdash*, The Holy Temple of Solomon.

---

41 Perkei Avot 1:2

As the clouds of dust and debris cleared, the stunned builders collected the pieces of their lives and followed the four winds. Among the survivors were the people of Javan, son of Japheth. Elishah, Tarshish, Kittim and Dodanim, all sons of Javan, migrated westward across Turkey, the Greek isles, Macedonia and on to the Italian Peninsula. They are of particular interest to us because their destiny is closely tied to the Roman Empire. Based on the linguistic and cultural similarities, the Kittim are generally thought to have also colonized Cyprus. Their cousins in the tribe of Elishah could have accompanied them.

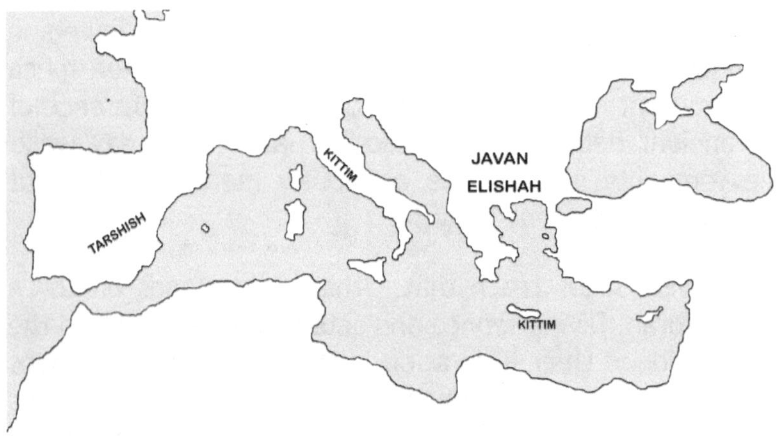

Elishah is echoed in the name of the inhabitants of the south coast of the island who were called Alashia.[42] Other sources suggest that the island colony was established on their way to Italy. In *Sefer HaYashar* we find an intriguing entry:

> And the children of Kittim (sic) are the Romim who dwell in the valley of Canopia by the River

[42] Anson F. Rainey and R .Steven Notley, *The Sacred Bridge* (Carta Books, Jerusalem, 2006) p. 27

Tibreu.[43]

Of course, the river is the Tiber on whose banks the city of Rome was built. We will again encounter these descendants in other sections of the book and how they impacted the descendants of Shem.

Those dispersed from the tower carried their Babel-bred ideologies with them as they separated into seventy nations. Their concept of Religion, Science and Government were a firmly entrenched aspect of their worldview. Nimrod also survived and even prospered, although he had achieved infamy for leading the people into folly. But he failed to mend his ways.

43 *Sefer HaYashar* 10:16

Chapter Six

ABRAHAM THE ICONOCLAST

The text of the Torah reveals little about the early years of Abraham; only that he was born as Abram to a man named Terah. He had an older brother called Haran. We also know that Abraham married the beautiful Sarai. In the next chapter of Genesis, we will read that HaShem instructed him to uproot his family and immigrate to a new land. Abraham is 75 years old when called to migrate.

This is amazing to consider. Abraham changed his way of life and relocated his family at an age when most men are contemplating the nearness of the grave. The fact that the Torah specifically mentions his age is a way of telling us that he was finally ready for his true mission. His whole life was in preparation for a new role.

What had molded Abraham's phenomenal character and made him fit for the task of becoming the father of nations?

There are hints of this process in the language of the Torah but we have to look to the Oral Torah to flesh out the formative experiences of his previous life. From these sources we learn that Terah, the father of Abraham, is a well-regarded and highly placed counselor to Nimrod. In fact, some sources state that Terah was actually the number two man in the kingdom, serving as Nimrod's viceroy.[44]

When Abraham was born, the seers warned Nimrod that the newborn of Terah would one day challenge Nimrod's claim of divinity. The king ordered Terah to bring the infant to the palace but Terah substituted a newborn belonging to one of his servants. Nimrod, believing that he held the son of Terah

---

[44] *The Torah Anthology*, Book One, p. 430

in his hands, slammed the child – headfirst – to the ground.

Terah took measures to conceal Abraham and his mother in a cave, sustaining them with daily provisions. Abraham remained hidden from the tyrant king until the age of ten, at which time he was sent to learn with Noah and Shem.

Before he was sent to these wise and righteous men, Abraham had already rejected idolatry at an early age. By observing the natural world around him, young Abraham reasoned that there was a Creator. He continued to grow under the profound influence of Noah and Shem; two people who had experienced the wonders and terrors of the previous world. As they continued to instill wisdom in their pupil and build Abraham's character, the tyrant Nimrod embarked on his infamous and ambitious Tower-building program.[45]

Abraham was 48 years old when the Tower of Babel fell. Some of the rabbinic commentaries mark it as the year that Abraham specifically acknowledged the idea of the one true G-d.[46]

Two more years passed and the future patriarch, secure in his faith, decided to return to his father's house in Ur. At that time, Terah was still one of Nimrod's staff officers. The failure of his tower project was a major setback, but Nimrod regrouped and probably moved his throne to the south; there he got back to the business of being a conqueror.

Abraham was shocked to find his father promoting idolatry. Thanks to his influence with the king, Terah was granted a license to run a successful side business as an idol maker. It is quite possible that he was fashioning images of Nimrod in

[45] Ibid., pp. 412-423

[46] *Codex Judaica*, p. 59

some form, along with other popular deities of the day including Shamash (the sun god) and Marduk. Terah worshipped twelve major deities representing each month, along with several minor ones.

Abraham realized that some visual display demonstrating the sheer folly of idolatry would have the most impact. He entered the inner sanctum of his father's house armed with an axe and demolished all of his father's wooden and stone icons – except one. Abraham then placed the axe into the outstretched arms of the remaining idol. As he exited the room, he encountered his father who had come to investigate the disturbance. Terah demanded an explanation; his son informed him that the statue holding the ax had destroyed all of the others. An incensed Terah spat back:

> Is there in these gods spirit, soul or power to do all that thou hast told me? Are they not wood and stone and have I not myself made them?[47]

Abraham asked Terah to consider the foolishness of his own words. He pleaded with him to give up his vain practices and follow the true G-d of the universe. When Terah refused to listen, Abraham grabbed the axe from the remaining icon and smashed it to pieces. Out of control with rage, Terah dragged his son to the palace so that he would face the wrath of the king.

During the extensive hearing that followed, Abraham used the proceedings as a forum to address those in attendance. He boldly challenged Nimrod and his followers to renounce their idolatrous customs. A shocked Nimrod realized that this young man was the promised child that he thought he had slain years ago. He demanded an explanation from Terah.

---

[47] *Sefer HaYashar* 11:42

Terah proved his treachery was boundless by claiming that his older son had engineered a charade – that it had been Haran's idea to substitute another infant in place of Abraham. Haran was seized and taken into custody.

It is also during this episode that we learn that Haran was never quite committed to the faith of Abraham. He equivocated. If his brother somehow prevailed against the king then he would publicly declare his obedience to Abraham's G-d. If the king prevailed, he would swear allegiance to him.

Orders were given to build a raging fire within a large furnace. All the inhabitants of Ur were invited to watch the execution of Abraham and Haran. The two brothers were stripped down to their undergarments and their hands bound with linen cords. The oven was so hot that the guards who thrust the two young men into the fire were immediately consumed. Haran was also burnt to death.

Abraham survived and stepped from the furnace.

Nimrod was stunned at the sight of Abraham emerging unscathed from the flames. He fell to his knees in front of the brave son of Terah. Abraham pleaded with the king and the awestruck crowds to worship only the one true G-d who created all things. Nimrod was so taken aback that he heaped honor and gifts upon Abraham, allowing him to live in peace.[48]

The Creator had other plans for the noble Abraham. In the space of two years, the goodwill between Nimrod and Abraham evaporated.

One restless night, Nimrod awakened in a cold sweat

---

[48] Rashi; *Bereshis Rabbah* 44:16, *Malbim*, also *Sefer HaYashar* 11:13-12:39

brought on by a disturbing dream. He called his counselors to explain the vivid nightmare in which he saw a figure resembling Abraham, stepping from a fiery furnace, wielding a sword and pursuing Nimrod along with three other kings. The distressed ruler demanded his counselors interpret the troubling vision. One advisor explained that Abraham would one day go to war and pursue Nimrod along with three allied leaders. The king would escape but one of Abraham's descendants would kill Nimrod in his old age.

The troubled monarch immediately dispatched troops to arrest Abraham. But he was warned by a young slave given to him by Nimrod. The figure we now know as the faithful Eliezar of Damascus had overheard Nimrod's advisers and slipped out of the palace to warn his master. Abraham eluded the king's men and escaped. His next stop was the home of Noah.

At this point, one might ask, why would Abraham worry? G-d had already saved him from being vaporized in the ovens of Kasdim. In part, Abraham felt responsible for the welfare of the several hundred people who had joined him. The Jewish sages teach that even a *tzadik*, a righteous person, never takes G-d for granted or waits for a miracle. One should do whatever is possible in any situation – only then, leave it to heaven. Terah, who had gained a new respect for his son had also made the journey. They arrived at the house of Noah and Shem and discussed what measures would insure their survival should Nimrod again relapse into paranoia.

The scene dazzles the mind as we visualize that meeting. On one side of the table, sat a man whose parents and grandparents actually knew Adam. Noah was that man and in the first six hundred years of his life, he had witnessed society descending into worldwide chaos. He oversaw the construction of a massive escape craft, stocked it with young animals and survived a terrifying global disaster. He founded a new world.[49] From the day that he boarded the ark until the small gathering in his home, just over 343 years had elapsed. He was now 940 years old.

Also on hand was Shem, who shared his father's epic experiences. As they counseled Abraham, they were fully aware that the time had come to usher in a new era for humankind; that the world was on the brink of redemption. Abraham could lead the way by raising the banner of righteousness and loving-kindness. He could disseminate the idea of ethical monotheism to all peoples.

Abraham was sure that the task could be accomplished – but may have believed that it could only happen if his family and friends moved away from the corrupting influences of Ur. The two antediluvian sages concurred. When the troops of Nimrod failed to locate Abraham, the mercurial dictator shelved the matter and returned to the business of expanding his empire. Unhindered by the despot, Abraham also expanded his small but vital following in Haran.

The Oral Tradition relates that Abraham lived an almost nomadic existence for the next twenty odd years as he moved between Haran and the land of Canaan. Many factors contributed to the commute. There was rampant unrest in the region from neighboring warlords attempting to wrest control from Nimrod and his expansive holdings. As mentioned previously, some events in the Torah are not always in chronological order and it is these years of the patriarch's life that this is most evident. Multiple promises to Abraham are strategically placed at key points in the Torah narrative, while in the Oral Tradition they are collectively repeated as Abraham shuttled his family between Haran and Canaan. For instance, while in his

[49] The *Mabbul* (Flood) began in the 600th year of Noah's life and the family disembarks from the ark after the passage of a year.

fifties, Abraham was still living in Haran when he is told:

> I am the Lord who brought thee forth from Ur Kasdim and delivered thee from the hands of thine enemies. And now, therefore if thou wilt hearken to my voice and keep my commandments, my statutes and my laws, then will I cause thy enemies to fall before thee, and I will multiply thy seed like the stars of heaven, and I will send my blessing upon all thy works and thou shalt lack nothing. Arise now, take thy wife and all belonging to thee and go to the land of Canaan and remain there, and I will there be unto thee for a God, and I will bless thee.[50]

After arriving in Canaan, the Creator spoke to him again and promised to make his descendants, "like the stars of heaven" and give them as "an inheritance all the lands which thou see."[51]

During Abraham's 58th year, Noah passed away at the age of 950. Abraham remained in Canaan until his 70th year. Again, the promises of G-d are restated to him, but he returned again for a short time to Haran. After staying for only five years, the patriarch, at the age of 75, was told by G-d, "*Lech Lecha* (go for yourself)."

The Written Torah does not introduce Abraham (as Abram) until the conclusion of chapter eleven in the book of Genesis.[52] The text offers scant details. Other than his lineage, we only learn that Abraham and his father Terah

---

50 *Sefer HaYashar* 13:3-5

51 Ibid., 13:7-8

52 Though the patriarch's name was not changed until later, we follow the rabbinic convention of referring to him as Abraham to honor him.

departed from Ur Kasdim bound for Canaan. But they only made it as far as Haran and settled there. The very next chapter opens with Abraham at the age of 75. The specific command to depart for Canaan was accompanied by promises of material and spiritual blessings, as well as a prophecy of nationhood. As detailed in *Sefer HaYashar*, there was a lot of migratory activity on the part of Abraham prior to his 75th year. The fact that the Torah mentions Abraham's age is significant.

First of all, the command came *directly* from HaShem. In *Sefer HaYashar,* he was informed of his destiny almost 25 years earlier but it is very likely that the words came from Noah and Shem as a prophecy. Yet, hearing from the Creator was a confirmation of both the source of the promises and an affirmation that he was truly in the Promised Land. It would also support the teaching that HaShem only communicates directly to those in *eretz* Israel.[53] The only exception to this was Moses, whose relationship with G-d was unique. Even though others in the *Tanakh* had heard from G-d, it is either through dreams, visions or *melakhim* (angelic messengers).

As previously noted in an earlier chapter, the other reason that the Torah mentions Abraham's age is that he had begun his genuine mission in life.

We may ask, why did Abraham seem to hesitate for over 25 years before finally settling in Canaan?

Part of the answer can be found in Genesis 11:32 which states that his father remained in Haran and died there. The verse seems to imply that Abraham waited until the death of Terah before he moved away. However, that is hardly the case.

---

[53] Hebrew phrase for "land of Israel."

Another detail regarding Terah, in that same verse, reveals that Terah died at the age of 205. That means when the 75-year-old Abraham moved to Canaan, and Terah lived for another 60 years! He was still around when his grandson, Isaac, reached the age of 35.[54] Therefore, his father was very much alive when Abraham settled in Canaan.

Why does the Torah then relate the age of his father and that he passes away in Haran?

The answer can be found in the Torah convention that the death of a person is stated because they no longer impact the narrative. Abraham was released from the influence of Terah. This is hinted at in the command, *Lech lecha,* which expresses more than just making one's way. According to Rabbi Samson Raphael Hirsch, *lech* is derived from a root that can also mean to *segregate* as in, "Go for yourself, sever your ties to your home, roots and father."[55]

Terah may have become a better person living in the sphere of his son's influence, but it was necessary for the mission of Abraham to actualize his full potential as the progenitor of a new nation. He had to separate himself from his past, even those in his family and their prevailing attitudes. The Hebrew of the text is concise and economic in explaining that this is a remarkable man who responds to an existential calling. Abraham began a fateful path that would bring forth a holy nation whose *Halacha* separates them from the world, for the sake of the world.

---

[54] *Sefer HaYashar* 21:6, records that Terah even journeyed from Haran to celebrate Isaac's birth.

[55] *The Hirsch Chumash, Sefer Bereshis*, p. 287

Chapter Seven

THE RISE OF EMPIRES

If we follow Abraham's trek through Canaan we see someone who appears to be surveying the entire region. His travels were interrupted by an extensive famine that sent him to Egypt. There, the pharaoh attempted to possess Sarah. The plagues that struck the king's palace precipitated the departure of Abraham with great riches bestowed by the pharaoh; an event that foreshadows the experiences of his descendants.

In an interesting side note, the Jewish historian Josephus tells us that the short time that Abraham spent among the Egyptians he gained their admiration by imparting to them his unique grasp of mathematics and astronomy.[56]

The patriarch returned to Canaan and settled with his kinsmen. They all prospered in peace, until a dispute erupted between Abraham and his nephew, Lot, over grazing rights. Abraham and Lot amicably parted ways. Lot moved to Sodom and Abraham settled at Mamre, near Hebron. It was after these events that the patriarch was forced to gather a militia to rescue his kidnapped nephew and becomes embroiled in an escalating regional war. It was a daring quest, but we tend to overlook the larger, fundamental principles established in this episode.

The narrative is another pattern of future events.

The kings listed in the first verses of Genesis 14 represent more than the warring cultures emerging from the rubble of

---

[56] *Antiquities of the Jews*, Book I, 8:2, translated by William Whiston, *The Life and Works of Flavius Josephus* (The John C. Winston Company, Philadelphia) p. 43

the Tower of Babel – they are the very foundation of the four world empires that will significantly impact Abraham, as well as his descendants, the people of Israel:

> And it happened in the days of Amraphel, king of Shinar; Arioch, king of Ellasar, Chedorlaomer, king of Elam, and Tidal, king of Goiim.
>
> – Genesis 14:1

The whole of the Levant was filled with blood and fury as these four monarchs overwhelmed other realms. Insurgency gave way to uneasy alliances followed by more conflicts. A confederation of five kings, based in Sodom and Gomorrah, revolted against the axis of four kings in Mesopotamia.

Chedorlaomer, the powerful Elamite monarch, Amraphel, Arioch and Tidal joined forces to mount a campaign to put down the rebellion by the five. Their armies met in the Valley of Siddim, at that time, a broad basin filled with tar pits. This geophysical feature is indicative of the unstable seismic nature of the region, which presaged the later destruction of the area and formation of the mineral-rich Dead Sea.

To the victors go the spoils and that included captives from the city of Sodom. Lot was among the prisoners taken by the four kings. When Abraham learned that his nephew had been taken, he assembled a war party of his compatriots and pursued the four kings and chased them to the far north of Canaan, in what later became the tribal portion of Dan. There, Abraham engaged them in combat. The pursuit finally ended at Chova, just north of Damascus where the armies were soundly defeated by Abraham.

Chedolaomer, Amraphel, Arioch and Tidal fled to their homes.

Abraham marched back to the south having reclaimed the spoils and the captives. The return was almost certainly along the King's Highway which bisected the region, running from Damascus down through the middle of Canaan. Patriarchs, prophets and conquerors all trod this historic path. Today, in Israel, much of that route is accessed by means of a modern highway.

Abraham continued southward and passed through the hills just east of Shalem, ruled by Melchizedek – better known as Shem, son of Noah.[57]

> He brought back all the property. He also brought back his kinsman Lot and all his goods, along with the women and the people. After he returned from his victory over Chedorlaomer and his allied kings, the king of Sodom came out to greet him in Shaveh Valley, now King's Valley. Malkhi-zedek, king of Salem, brought forth bread and wine. He was a priest to God, the Most High.
>
> – Genesis 14:16- 18

This entire incident, beginning with the attempted conquest by the Four Kings to the resolution with Abraham, was much more than a raucous military skirmish – it was a turning point in the history of the world.

The reader will note that one of the four monarchs was called Amraphel–another name for Nimrod.[58] There is an enlightening discussion, in the *Talmud*, between Rabbi Abba Arikha (known simply as Rav) and Rabbi Samuel Yahina'ah (Shmuel). Rav argued that Nimrod was the actual name of

---

[57] All the sages identify Shem as Melchizedek. See the *Artscroll Tanakh, Bereishis* Vol.1a (Mesorah Publications, Brooklyn, NY 1988) p. 493

[58] The *Talmud, Eruvin 53a*, also notes that Amraphel is derived from *am* (people) and *rophel* (to fall) and means "he caused the people to fall."

the tyrant while Shmuel countered by pointing out that the name is only evocative since it is derived from *merod*, meaning "to rebel," and therefore it was not his real name. If Nimrod is a corruption of his real name, it would be in keeping with the commandment not to utter or write the name of an idol.[59]

There is much evidence to suggest that Nimrod may have been known by another name or title. Amraphel could be a corruption or pun derived from Hammurabi. Famous for the Code of Hammurabi, this ancient ruler is thought to have arrived much later than the era of Abraham. The name could have been bestowed on successive heirs who took his throne.

Though Hammurabi is famous for establishing some of the first laws in history, their very harshness suggests a Nimrod-like ruler. Infractions such as harboring a runaway slave, refusing military service or theft were all punishable by death.[60]

Hammurabi was actually called Ammurapi. H. W. F. Sagg, author of *The Babylonians*, notes that Ammurapi "was probably pronounced Khammurapi."[61] If Nimrod and Khammurapi are one and the same, then the latter appellation is surely a surname that incorporates and honors *Kham*, known to most English readers as Ham, the grandfather of Nimrod.[62] Saggs states that Khammurapi was

[59] Exodus 23:13 "Be careful to do everything I have said to you. Do not invoke the names of other gods; do not let them be heard on your lips."

[60] *The Code of Hammurabi King of Babylon*, Robert Francis Harper (Univ. of Chicago Press, 1904)

[61] H. W. F. Sagg, *The Babylonians* (Folio Society, London, 1999) pp. 62-63

[62] The Hebrew pronunciation is spelled with *het* giving it a guttural 'h' sound.

the greatest ruler of Babylon's First Dynasty and created a realm larger than modern Iraq. There is an additional linguistic connection between Ammurapi and Amraphel allowed by exchangeable "p" sound and "f" sound as found in the Semitic tongue. It is quite plausible that the Torah is denying this rogue any honor by altering Ammurapi into a pun, calling him Amraphel, literally "he caused the people to fall." It was Nimrod/Amraphel who organized the people at Shinar, or Sumer, the very foundation of the Babylonian Empire and its first dynasty.

Chedorlaomer was the head of the Elamite mountain clans that later developed into the Persian Empire. Prior to the building of the Tower, he was a prince serving under the leadership of Nimrod. After the dispersion from the Babel, Chedorlaomer rebelled against Nimrod and led a contingent to settle the land between what is now Iraq and Iran. It is likely, that he is known to us in historical accounts as *Kudurmabuk* of Larsa.[63]

Arioch was the leader of Ellasar. The name suggests Elishah, the son of Javan and ancestor of the Ionians or Greeks. A son of Javan, Elishah could be another form of Ellasar. Elishah is progenitor of the Hellenes, another name for the Greeks. Elisha is probably the source for the name of the place called the Elysian Fields.[64] These linguistic clues link Arioch to the earliest beginnings of ancient Greece.

Tidal was called king of Goiim and is thought to be the ruler that historians call *Tudhalia*, a Hittite king. According to the lengthy Torah commentary known as *MeAm Lo'Ez*, Tidal led a collective of nations. This source also notes that Goiim was

[63] *The Babylonians*, p. 62

[64] *Antiquities of the Jews*, Book One, Chapter 6:1, p. 40

a site located on the Italian Peninsula.[65] This suggests that the culture would eventually be a component of the Roman Empire.

Note how this account of Abraham's clash with these four titans reveals a marvelous foreshadowing of world events. One man, the progenitor of the Jewish nation, and his small army of faithful take on the founders of Babylon, Persia, Greece and Rome and defeated them. Abraham's experience with the four kings is more evidence that the lives of the forefathers foreshadow the experiences of their descendants. Abraham's bold move against the four monarchs is a prophetic vision of how his descendants, the nation of Israel (the smallest of people) would survive and outlast enormous empires that attempted to absorb and erase them.

As we shall see, there will be continued references to these four empires throughout the Bible and in commentaries from the Jewish Sages.

Piece Pact

The fifteenth chapter of Genesis tells of the *Brit Bein HaBetarim*, the Covenant Between the Pieces. The placement of this divine accord immediately after Abraham's victory over the Four kings reveals that the two events – though not in chronological order – are linked in a very profound way. It begins as a dialogue between the Abraham and the Creator:

> "I am the Lord, who brought you out of Ur of the Chaldeans to give you this land for a possession." But Abram said, "My Lord G-d, how can I know that I will gain possession of it?"

---

[65] *Torah Anthology*, Vol 2, Genesis, p. 50

— Genesis 15:7-8

G-d responded with a set of instructions. He told Abraham to perform burnt offerings with five types of kosher animals. He divided them, except for the small birds, and placed the pieces opposite each other. In addition to slaughtering the animals and preparing them for sacrifice, he had to fight off scavenger birds. Just before sunset he slumped into an exhausted, troubled sleep:

> ...a thick and dreadful darkness came over him. Then the Lord said to him, "Know for certain that your descendants will be strangers in a country not their own, and they will be enslaved and mistreated four hundred years. But I will punish the nation they serve as slaves, and afterward they will come out with great possessions. You, however, will go to your fathers in peace and be buried at a good old age. In the fourth generation your descendants will come back here, for the sin of the Amorites has not yet reached its full measure."
>
> — Genesis 15:13-16

This extraordinary prophetic vision concluded with a smoking furnace, and a fiery torch that passed between the pieces. The sages have generated pages of insightful commentaries on this revelation and its stunning imagery — how it encompasses the whole of Jewish history. Though layered with profound teachings, I will focus on only two aspects.

First of all, the placement of this particular narrative in the Torah comes on the heels of Abraham's victory, confirming that his dealings with the Four Kings will have consequences for his descendants. The sages inform us that Abraham's descendants, because of their need to develop character, cast off negative traits and mature into leaders, would also experience trials. The patriarch was asked to choose what kind of trials his descendants should face and Abraham believed that the most suitable method would be to allow them to learn via the rigors of history. His decision then prompted the thick vision of darkness which was an allusion to the smothering subjugation of the Babylonian, Greek, Persian and Roman empires.

Secondly, and just as crucial, was the actual covenant itself – the legal instrument by which the Creator bequeaths the Promised Land.

G-d also invoked the powerful visuals that accompanied the Covenant Between the Pieces to introduce another player who would take on the task of molding Abraham's progeny with far more zeal than necessary. Of course, the player is Egypt. It is the nation G-d will punish – the one that Israel *"will serve as slaves,"* referenced in Genesis 15:14. This part of the divine sound and light show is actually the answer to the patriarch's original question, *"How will I know I'm going to inherit this land?"*

What he saw in the swirling darkness before him must have prompted the question asked by every Jewish child throughout history. Abraham surely viewed the blackness of each empire as separate nights of history and beheld the terrible oppression and asked, "Why is this night different than all the other nights?" And the reply resonates with us today: Abraham's seed endured a four-century exile with various degrees of domination and servitude that culminated in miraculous emancipation that was a sign of the inheritance. This then is how we know today that the land of Israel is the birthright of the Jewish People because they experienced both the tears of exile in Egypt and the miracles of the Exodus.

The 400 year period began with the birth of Isaac, 30 years after G-d made this pact with Abraham. The vital linkage between the Exodus saga and the Covenant Between the Pieces is their common date. The covenant was made on the 15th day of Nissan – the very day that Israel would observe their first Passover on the eve of their celebrated departure from Egypt.

Chapter Eight

THE *AKEIDAH*

Abraham's campaign against the Four Kings was his fifth test or trial. *Perkei Avot* (Ethics of the Fathers) states that there were ten trials in all. There is a slight difference of opinion as to what the ten were. For instance, the Rambam lists the second test as the famine in Canaan that sent Abraham to Egypt, while Rashi states it was literally the trial by fire when he was thrown into the oven by Nimrod. However, the sages all agree that the tenth and final test was the Binding of Isaac, known as the *Akeidah,* which unfolds in Chapter 22 of Genesis. This is only time that Torah actually tells us that G-d tested the patriarch. The Hebrew word for test can also mean exalted. It was time for Abraham to enter a higher level in his relationship with G-d. It also meant that the Creator was going to fulfill part of his promise to Abraham years earlier that he would, "make him great." It all begins with a three-day journey with his son Isaac:

> When they finally came to the place designated by God, Abraham built the altar there, and arranged the wood. He then bound his son Isaac, and placed him on the altar on top of the wood. Abraham took the knife to slit his son's throat. God's angel called to him from heaven and said, "Abraham! Abraham!" "Yes," he replied. "Do not harm the boy. Do not do anything to him. For now I know that you fear God. You have not withheld your only son." Abraham looked up and saw a ram caught by its horns in a thicket. He got the ram, offering it in his son's place. Abraham named the place "God will See" [*Adonai Yir'eh*]. Today, it is therefore said, "On God's Mountain, He will be seen." God's angel called to Abraham from

> heaven a second time, and said, "God declares, 'I have sworn by My own Essence, that because you performed this act, and did not hold back your only son, I will bless you greatly, and increase your offspring like the stars of the sky and the sand on the seashore. Your offspring shall inherit their enemies' gate. All the nations of the world shall be blessed through your descendant because you obeyed My voice.'"
>
> — Genesis 22:9-18

The reader can readily see, in this episode, the template that anticipates the Sinai experience of the Chosen People:

- Abraham must journey to a mountain.
- Ishmael and Eliezer, symbolic of the *Erev Rav* (Mixed Multitude), are also on hand.
- The Patriarch sees the mountain topped with a pillar of smoke.
- Abraham offers his son to HaShem.
- An animal is sacrificed instead of the son.

It is only a recent development that the English translations of the Torah have reflected a more accurate understanding of its content. The story of the *Akeidah* is a good example. The Hebrew text never states that Abraham was commanded to slaughter Isaac — only to bring "the son that he loved" for an offering at the very same place Noah offered a sacrifice after surviving the Flood. Abraham was also aware that the site would be the future location of the Temple sacrifices. Yet, he was so unswerving in his faith and so obedient to G-d, he was ready to carry out what he believed was the command as he understood it. Isaac, no mere lad, but a man who had just turned 37, also understood.[66]

It was only after the ram was sacrificed that he realized the role of his children in the scheme of the Creator's grand plan. Those ashes smoldering on the altar were actually a dramatic affirmation of life. It was also evidence of the faith of HaShem in His people. From that point on, the Creator would "see" the ashes of the firstborn. The site is even called *Yerih-shalem* or "G-d will see." We still know it by that name today.

The Creator viewed Abraham's intent as absolutely authentic because the patriarch was thoroughly convinced that Isaac would perish. Abraham's feeling of imminent loss was genuine. He was convinced he would see his son die. The contemporary Western mind is frustrated by the written narrative of the *Akeidah*. It seems to create more questions than it answers. But the quality of the narrative is a lesson in itself. By not providing easy answers, G-d is demonstrating that His people must always maintain that state of mind known as *emunah*, or trust. The *Akeidah* was the turning point that represented a unique individual's unwavering commitment to G-d. It flowered at Sinai when a unique multitude made their commitment to the Creator. The latter mountain was the culmination of a promise made to Abraham when he began his mission in life:

> I will make you into a great nation. I will bless you and make you great. You shall become a blessing.
>
> — Genesis 12:2

It was a promise actualized when G-d took the Twelve Tribes out of Egypt and led them to a mountain located in a desolate patch of ground that no kingdom claimed:

[66] *Codex Judaica*, p. 64

> You will be a kingdom of priests and a holy nation to Me.
>
> — Exodus 19:6

The Torah was given to both instruct Israel and to sanction explicit laws for every facet of their life, for example, the daily sacrifices. They were carried out in a defined manner. The *halacha*, literally the way to walk, preserves the sanctity of the commandments and prevents the introduction of extraneous or foreign elements. This stringency is no different than, for example, the precision required to assemble a structure or to formulate a prescription. If a construction crew ignores the blueprint, the building will not resemble the original design and may not even stand. If specific ingredients and measures are ignored for a compound, it will fail to produce the desired results.

The creation of Israel represented a unique partnership in which G-d provides the necessities crucial for a life of sacrifice to G-d and humanity by a nation of priests called Israel. The being of every Jew is rooted in the *Akeidah*, a model of utter, selfless service to the Creator. In a later chapter, we will investigate how the Torah and Christianity view the *Akeidah* in powerfully diametric ways.

Chapter Nine

SOUL FOOD

> The lore has not died out of the world, and you will still find people who believe that soup will cure any hurt or illness, and is no bad thing to have for the funeral either.
>
> — John Steinbeck, *East of Eden*

Genesis, chapter 25, tells of the death of Abraham. It also describes how Isaac and Ishmael came together to bury their father, a detail imbued with prophetic promise that in the latter days their descendants would unite. The reaction to Abraham's passing at the age of 175, and the scope of the mourning, gives us some sense of the influence of the great patriarch. His internment resembled a state funeral in Hebron with the great and small from Canaan gathered to pay their respects.[67]

But there was a notable absence among the mass of mourners in attendance at Hebron. It was Esau. He had gone hunting instead. It was act of borne of bitterness as related in narrative found in the Torah commentary *MeAm Lo'ez:*

> "Now I see," said Esau, "that there is no Judge or justice. Abraham was the greatest saint who ever lived. He kept God's commandments as well as humanly possible. Still, he did not even live as long as Noah or other early generations. I therefore see that religion has no value."[68]

---

[67] The original English version of *Sefer HaYashar*, translated in 1840, is available as *The Authentic Annals of the Early Hebrews*, aka the *Book of Jasher*, aka *Sefer HaYashar*, compiled by Wayne Simpson (Lightcatcher Books, Springdale, AR, 2003) p. 54-56

[68] *Torah Anthology*, Genesis Vol. II, p. 466

Of course, the sad truth is revealed that Esau did not really see the truth. What he "saw" was an excuse to run amok because of the death of someone that he deeply respected. That he would decide to go hunting reveals his contaminated spiritual connection to another infamous hunter:

> He acted like Nimrod. Hence it is written, Like
>
> Nimrod a mighty hunter before the Lord.
>
> – Midrash Rabbah 37:2

Nimrod and Esau have a fateful encounter following the death of Abraham. At that time, Nimrod's superstardom is somewhat diminished since the failure of his Tower project but he still ruled a kingdom. Esau spies an entourage led by Nimrod and conceals himself. He had good reason to avoid the leader. The reputation of Esau's prowess as a hunter and his popularity was a source of concern for Nimrod who was convinced that he might have political ambitions.

> And Nimrod was observing Esau all his days, for jealousy formed in the heart of Nimrod against Esau all the days.[69]

This particular encounter provided Esau with an opportunity to steal something from Nimrod that was highly prized. It was the famous cloak of Adam. You may recall the description of this remarkable garment in Chapter Four. It was the part of the wardrobe made by G-d and given to Adam and Eve after their expulsion from *Gan Eden*. It was passed down to the antediluvian patriarchs and later stolen by Ham. He had removed it from the Ark and entrusted it to Cush who then bestowed it to Nimrod.

---

[69] Ibid., p. 56-57

Esau waited until Nimrod dispatched his men to the outer perimeter of the camp. He sprang from his hiding place, beheaded Nimrod and removed the legendary cloak. The bloodshed continued when Esau was surprised by the returning attendants and killed them. The remaining troops launched a search for the unknown assassin, but Esau escaped undetected. He breathlessly returned home. Here, we return to the epic narrative in the Torah that relates the following in almost terse language:

> Jacob simmered a stew, and Esau came from the field, and he was exhausted. Esau said to Jacob, "Pour into me, now, some of that very red stuff for I am exhausted." (He therefore called his name Edom.) Jacob said, "Sell, as this day, your birthright to me." Esau said, "Look, I am going to die, so of what use is a birthright?" Jacob said, "Swear to me as this day;" he swore to him and sold his birthright to Jacob. Jacob gave Esau bread and lentil stew, and he ate and drank, got up and left; Esau spurned his birthright.
>
> – Genesis 25:29-33

Jacob was cooking lentils, the traditional dish for those in mourning. He would have been preparing the meal for his father, following the funeral of Abraham. The Hebrew text is dense with prophetic insights that expose the nature of Esau. The stew is described as red, the color that stained Esau to his very core – to the degree he was given the name Edom. The soup enticed him because it reminded him of the blood he spilled in the hunt. As we shall see in later chapters, red banners would fly over the armies of conquering nations that sprang from his loins and they would soak the earth with the blood they would spill.[70]

[70] Curiously, the land called Edom has always bordered the shores of the Red Sea.

His penchant for instant gratification is highlighted by the use of "now" rendered from the Hebrew *nah*. Although the word can imply "please," in this case it was more likely to signify "raw" – indicating that Esau wanted the soup before it was finished. He drained the soup in one greedy gulp. The fact that the sale is detailed with such brevity is a clue in itself – symbolic of how little regard Esau had for the birthright. Esau was convinced that the murder of Nimrod would be discovered and his death would surely follow.

The Oral Torah tells us that Esau and Jacob were only fifteen years old on that very day.[71] The age of the twins suggest that the transaction was nothing more than an adolescent prank.[72] But only Esau held this view. Surely, he thought, Jacob can't seriously believe that I would sell my birthright? Esau viewed the whole transaction as nothing more than a joke, which explains his bewildered astonishment when, years later, he discovered Jacob had the *chutzpah* to actually seek the blessing of the firstborn.

In their brief transaction we can easily see a profound and existential gulf between the brothers. Following the death of their beloved grandfather, Jacob went home and prepared a meal for the mourners, while Esau indulged in his favorite pastime.

Isaac chose to ignore the dangerous flaws in Esau, but Jacob saw him for the scoundrel he was. He understood that Esau could never sustain the Abrahamic legacy that would one day yield a holy nation of priests. He ignored the pain of others, then glibly agreed to bargain away his birthright for a bowl of soup. Ultimately, it was the sale that convinced

---

[71] The twins were born 2108 on the Hebrew calendar. The death of Abraham and the sale of the birthright occurred in the year 2123, thus Jacob and Esau would have been 15 years old – see *Codex Judaica*, p. 64

[72] *Talmud, Bava Batra* 16b

Jacob that his brother lacked a vital leadership quality – Esau was not a man of his word.

> Jacob said, "Swear to me this day," so he swore and sold him his birthright.
>
> – Genesis 25:33

To Jacob, his word was his bond. He asked his brother to swear *ki'yom*, "like the day." In other words, this transaction is as real as the day. Esau, skilled at telling people what they wanted to hear, agreed. Indeed, to Esau who "trapped men with his mouth," talk was cheap. This aspect of Esau reveals his connection to Nimrod. The sages tell us that the infamous tyrant was the first person to be a king after the Flood. Rashi and many other commentators affirm that Nimrod beguiled men with his words. Rav Hirsch describes him as the model for history's hypocrites who wrap themselves in piety so they can lead the people astray.[73]

Nimrod was the first politician and Esau was his apt pupil.

The *bechorah*, or birthright, carried certain privileges but also important responsibilities. At the father's passing, the eldest became head of the household which, by the way, also meant bringing the sacrifices. The firstborn son received a greater portion of the inheritance. There were practical considerations for giving the eldest son a generous share. This largesse provided the resources to lead and care for the family of the late father. The vital role of the firstborn son and its attendant blessings is underscored by the importance that G-d placed on the position. In His role as the ultimate Father, the Creator instructed Moses, at the burning bush:

---

[73] *Interlinear Chumash*, Commentary on Genesis 10:8-10 (Mesorah Publications, Brooklyn, NY 2006) p. 51

> You shall say to Pharaoh, "so said HaShem, My firstborn son is Israel."
>
> — Exodus 4:22

This verse makes it abundantly clear that G-d chose the Jews to be priests of His household. They are to be the elder brother with all of the responsibilities of the firstborn, including care of the younger siblings — in essence, the rest of humanity.

Esau was schooled at the knee of Isaac in the deepest secrets of the ancient knowledge. One day that wisdom would be bequeathed, in the form of the Torah, to his descendants. Yet Esau did not embrace these tenets. He chafed at his father's lifestyle and found it restrictive and unrewarding.

Esau understood the meaning of his name and saw himself as complete and needing nothing from anyone. He was a perfectionist. Everything and everyone had to conform to Esau's standards. Thus, he lacked compassion or *chesed*:

> It is no wonder then, that Eisav committed crimes of violence. The striving for perfection inevitably leads to the ultimate anti-chesed — brute force.[74]

The role model provided by Nimrod as world builder was far more appealing to the ambitious Esau. Recall how the tower was constructed under Nimrod's direction. The Torah sets the stage for massive undertaking by telling us:

> The people were of one speech and one

[74] Batya Gallant, *Stages of Spiritual Growth* (Devora Publishing, Jerusalem / NY, 2010) p.63

> purpose.[75]

The reader will also recall how the word "speech" is translated from *saphah* meaning completion *but also limitation*. Though not the same, the word is very similar to the meaning of Esau's name and connects him to the philosophy of the Tower generation. Nimrod and those who departed from *Shinar* still embodied the concept expressed in *saphah*. It was evident in their conviction that armed power and intellect would sustain them completely. They believed they were world builders, but tragically limited in the ability to complete their dream because of their rejection of Divine wisdom.

The source of this philosophy was Cain. His ideology survived the Flood and was carried into the new world by Ham who passed it on to Caanan and then Nimrod. It was Esau's natural inclination to be dazzled by the trappings of power enjoyed by Nimrod. This explains, in part, why Esau rejected the more meaningful, but intangible rewards of his father's ways. It does not matter that Esau did not believe that he had actually sold away his inheritance. The sale of the birthright is a spiritual DNA strand spiraling right back to Cain and Abel.

Esau, like Cain, only valued that which he could touch, taste and see while Jacob prized the ethereal and the supernal. Esau had his eye on the material possessions of his father Isaac. Rabbi Samson Raphael Hirsch sums up the significance of their transaction:

> Just as then they stood opposed to each other, so will Jacob stand opposed to Esav throughout the centuries. Jacob will willingly give up his material possessions to Esav, who craves them, if the latter

[75] Genesis 11:1

> will only allow him to attend to his spiritual and moral mission.[76]

We still have to ask, how could Esau remain unaffected by the influence of two parents like Isaac and Rebecca?

The first answer is the most obvious – Free Will.

But there is additional insight into the mind of Esau and his rejection of the righteous for the riotous. The answer is available to us in a simple phrase found in Genesis 25:28:

> Isaac loved Esau, for his hunt was in his mouth, but Rebecca loved Jacob.

These words are a poignant reminder that the Torah does not flinch in revealing the revered Biblical figures were subject to very human faults. Instead of loving and instructing the boys in equal measure, Isaac and Rebecca treated the twins very differently. Isaac rightly believed that the boisterous vitality of Esau was essential for leadership, as Rabbi Abraham Isaac HaKohen Kook tells us:

> Isaac appreciated Esau's ability to hunt and dominate the beasts, the trait needed to dominate bestial peoples. [77]

Isaac may have feared that tempering Esau's innate vitality might break his spirit. In one respect, it happened anyway, but the opposite occurred. The passionate physicality of Esau eventually quenched his spiritual side. Rebecca embraced the kinder, gentler Jacob and nurtured the divine spark she saw in him. The twins possessed G-d-given

---

[76] *The Hirsch Chumash, Sefer Bereshis,* p. 563

[77] Kook, *Gold From the Land of Israel,* translated by Rabbi Chanan Morrison (Urim Publications, Jerusalem & New York, 2006) p. 62

attributes unique to them. However, Isaac and Rebecca failed to cultivate those qualities in equal measure. The misstep of these venerable parents is recorded for the best of reasons – instruction. Lawrence Kelemen is a proponent of developing parental skills drawn from this timeless wisdom of the Torah. In his *To Kindle a Soul*, Kelemen speaks of the Torah's balanced approach to child-rearing, characterizing it as "planting and building." The method of instilling necessary qualities by "building" brings immediate, observable changes in a child while "planting" yields results more slowly but more permanently.

Kelemen speaks of the value of both methods. His warnings of planting without building (or structure) sounds eerily like a formula for raising an Esau:

> We must sow seeds of compassion and nobility, tend them, and faithfully wait while human greatness sprouts forth. However, planting alone will produce a wild, undirected, ultimately fruitless vine. A child deprived of structure will become a wild adult.[78]

If we carry the analogy of planting even further we could say that as a parent who is watering and tending these tender plants we call our children, we have an opportunity to affect their growth so that they arrive at maturity with as few flaws as possible. Ultimately, Esau and not his parents, is responsible for his actions as an adult. Whatever hindrances may have been put in his path---even by his parents---does not negate the Free Will that would have allowed him to overcome those hurtles and become worthy of the mantle of leadership.

---

78 Lawrence Kelemen, *To Kindle A Soul* (Targum Press, Southfield, MI, 2001) p. 31

Chapter Ten

THE HOLY CHARADE

The impact of the birthright sale will not be felt until years later when Jacob and Esau are 63. That transaction culminates in one of the most misunderstood narratives in the Torah – the so-called "stolen blessing."

This episode is set in motion in the same manner as the sale of the *bechorah*: Esau on the hunt and the preparation of a meal. Isaac, feeling the aches and pains of his age and thinking he might die soon, decided it may be time to pass along the mantle of leadership to his son. Even though he was 123 at this point in his life, Isaac lived on for another 15 years.[79]

What could have caused him to suddenly dwell on the transience of life? Some of the commentaries suggest that Isaac felt this way because his mother, Sarah, had died at the age of 127 and he was approaching that milestone. We can all relate to that sudden sense of our own mortality. Another reason for his decision was because Isaac knew that it was an auspicious time for the blessing. That day was the anniversary of the *Brit Bein HaBetarim*, the Covenant Between the Pieces.

In addition to his advanced years, Isaac was blind. This is a literal and symbolic description. His failing eyesight prevented him from seeing the debauchery of the Esau. As a "trapper of men with his mouth" he had also ensnared Isaac. Hearing the voice of Esau spouting oratory caused Isaac to be blind to his son's true nature.

Isaac called out to Esau, asking him to take up his hunting

---

[79] *Torah Anthology,* Genesis Vol. II, p. 486

gear, bring home some game and prepare his favorite food, "that he may bless him." The Torah records that Esau replied, *hineni*, which is usually translated as "here am I."

Every time this phrase appears in the Torah, something crucial in the development of the Chosen People is about to take place.

Rabbi Samson Raphael Hirsch notes that Isaac's promise to bless Esau for carrying out his request is not a promise of reward for doing a good deed; rather it was Isaac's intent that Esau realize that his obvious physical skills – for that matter, any skill – can be elevated in the service of G-d by showing kindness to another. Rebecca had overheard the entire exchange and summoned Jacob to bring two goats from their flock so that she could cook up a feast.[80] Rebecca wanted Jacob to serve the meat to his father so that he would receive the blessing instead of Esau. When Jacob objected that such trickery could backfire, his mother assured him, "The curse be upon me."

Rebecca spoke with such confidence because she obviously had it on the best authority that Jacob, as the younger of the twins, must receive the blessing. The reader will recall that she was informed by G-d while she carried the boys in her womb:

> ...and the elder shall serve the younger.
>
> – Genesis 25:23

These prophetic words echoed in Rebecca's ears as she dressed Jacob in the "costly garments" of Esau – the robes fashioned by G-d for Adam and very same royal finery Esau

80 There is a definite connection between these goats and the two later used in the *Yom Kippur* service.

had removed from the body of Nimrod 48 years earlier.[81] The masquerade was complete when Rebecca strapped the skins from the slaughtered goats onto the hands, arms and neck of Jacob. He carried the food to his father and announced his presence.

It is at this point, that most translations fail to accurately convey Jacob's conversation with his father. The English interpretation would have us believe that Jacob blatantly claimed to be Esau. According to Rashi, Jacob's words to his father as recorded in Genesis 27:19 should be rendered:

> It is I who bring this to you. Esau is your firstborn.[82]

In fact, the whole exchange between father and son is purposely ambiguous. Isaac, unable to discern the face of the figure before him, asked his son to come closer. Isaac had no reason to suspect it was anyone other than Esau, since it was only his eldest that he had asked to trap wild game, whip up a tasty repast and be blessed. When Jacob drew near, Isaac reacted as if something was amiss because he heard:

> ...the voice of Jacob but the hands are the hands of Esau.
>
> — Genesis 27:22

We may think that the voice was different than Esau's but, to the contrary, the sages record that, since they were twins, they sounded very much alike. However, it was Jacob's manner of expression — his choice of words — that set him apart from

---

[81] *Bereshith Rabbah* II (Socino Press, London, NY, 1983) p. 592. Also see *Codex Judaica*, p. 61

[82] *Interlinear Chumash* (Mesorah Publications, Brooklyn, NY 2006) p. 149

his brother. Isaac inquired again if the son he embraced was Esau. Jacob continued to evade a direct statement and only replied, "It is I."

Isaac dispensed with further questions. Even so, he may still have had doubts. When the meal was finished, Isaac asked his son to come close so that he could kiss him. Isaac breathed in the odor of the garments worn by Jacob:

> He approached and kissed him. Isaac smelled the fragrance of his garments, and blessed him. He said, "See, my son's fragrance is like the perfume of a field blessed by G-d. May G-d grant you the dew of heaven and the fat of the earth, much grain and wine. Nations will serve you; governments will bow down to you. You shall be like a lord over your brother; your mother's children will prostrate themselves to you. Those who curse you are cursed and those who bless you are blessed."
>
> – Genesis 27:27-29

At this point, many of us are shaking our heads wondering how Isaac could have been so easily duped. He was in denial.

In the previous chapter, the Torah relates a seemingly normal event. Years earlier, at the age of 40, Esau married two Hittite women, Judith and Basemath, described in the Oral Tradition as idol worshippers. It had a profound effect on his parents:

> Esau's wives became a source of spiritual bitterness to Isaac and Rebecca.
>
> – Genesis 26:34-35

The very next chapter is the story of the blessing of Jacob. It begins with a description of Isaac as aged and blind. The juxtaposition of the verses is significant, signifying that Isaac was in denial – he chose to not see Esau's ways. No one was more aware of this than his wife Rebecca. Her ruse reads like a poor charade because that's what it was. Rebecca, in her wisdom, was accomplishing twin goals in putting on what Rabbi Samson Raphael Hirsch describes as a clumsy comedy. Rav Hirsch is not casting aspersions, and goes on to remind us of Rebecca's greatness; he points out that Rebecca was well aware that a sizzling pot roast and hairy gloves would never deceive her husband. Her costume sham demonstrated that Esau's sanctimonious façade was just as clumsy and never fooled anyone. But could there have been an additional motive?

I would like to suggest that she may have used this bit of theater to prevent Esau from taking the blessing while providing Isaac an out – allowing him to make a "mistake" and bestowing the blessing on Jacob. This might explain why Isaac seemed to play along, especially after hearing such obvious evasions from his younger son, Jacob.

The Torah does contain history, but its paramount function for the Jewish people is to serve as an all-encompassing, timeless book of instruction designed to re-shape worlds. Seemingly mundane details can access deeper teachings. We can draw additional insight from this curious picture of Jacob donning a costume and pretending to be his older brother. The clue can be found in Isaac's reaction when he heard the speech pattern of Jacob but felt the hands of Esau. The words of Jacob had given his father pause. Rashi says that Jacob honored the Creator in his speech – something Esau rarely did. Author Ken Spiro, in his *Crash Course in Jewish History* explains why this reference to Jacob's voice is so profound:

> What does "the voice" symbolize? Speech is

> uniquely human. Animals may communicate, but they cannot speak or express abstract ideas. Speech is therefore representative of spirituality and intellect.[83]

There is another aspect to the use of speech in this context. Esau, though known for his articulate manner, used the power of words for his own gain and to entrap people. Referencing the voice of Jacob and the hands of Esau draws attention to the distinctive persona of each brother and teaches a compelling, vibrant lesson to the Jewish people: The mission of Israel and the key to their survival requires that they take on external qualities such as strength, daring and boldness – positive attributes of Esau. At the same time, they must always speak with the voice of Jacob, which means speaking words of Torah. Israel is Jacob, the inner man of G-d, motivated by a holy mission but clothed in the physical power necessary to establish a holy nation and, ultimately be a shining example to all other nations on the earth.

Back to the Garden

There, in that quiet warmth of Isaac's room in Beersheba, on the 15th day of the month we now call Nissan, something monumental had just taken place. We know this because of a curious phrase in the blessing by Isaac when he described "a field blessed by G-d." The consensus among Jewish commentators is that this as an allusion to *Gan Eden*, the Garden of Eden. It is no mere coincidence that the words appear at this point in the Biblical narrative. This remarkable reference is a portal that sends the reader hurtling back through the centuries to the first estate of

---

[83] Ken Spiro, *Crash Course in Jewish History* (Targum Press, Southfield, MI 2010)
p. 29

humanity. The Torah is directing our attention to Adam and Eve. There is a direct association between their fall and the blessing given to Jacob. Both events share common elements but with very different outcomes.

Adam and Eve were told by G-d that they must not eat the fruit from the Tree of Knowledge, Good and Evil. The words of the *naHash* led Eve to doubt the words of the Creator. She took the forbidden fruit and convinced Adam to do the same. Their eyes were opened. They were expelled from the Garden but, to protect them, the Creator fashioned garments of skin. G-d told Eve she would experience pain in childbirth. This reference to painful pregnancy directly links her to Rebecca. And, like Eve, she delivered twins.

The Torah is telling us these women were spiritually connected.

Marvelously, things changed in Rebecca's day. Instead of being deceived, Rebecca deceived her husband and "opens his eyes" to see his error. She accomplished this with a masquerade utilizing garments of skin.

The effect of this holy charade was that the plan of G-d took a quantum leap forward.

While Eve doubted the Creator, Rebecca held His words in her heart – determined the spiritual mantle would pass to the worthy son. Jacob, too, is recognized for joining his mother in rectifying the sin of Adam and Eve:

> He conquered the snake by means of deception, *middah kenegged middah*.[84] The snake used deception to bring curses upon the world. Yaakov Avinu used deception for the sake of heaven and

[84] "Measure for measure"

> was thereby able to regain blessings for the world, those very same blessings the snake denied us.[85]

Jacob would eventually be given the name Israel and called firstborn by the Creator because the blessing bestowed upon on him was no less than a re-birth.

> Nations will serve you; governments will bow down to you. You shall be like a lord over your brother; your mother's children will prostrate themselves to you. Those who curse you are cursed, and those who bless you are blessed.
>
> – Genesis 27:29

By accepting this noble calling, he restored the plan that started in *Gan Eden* – the plan for a priesthood, serving the Creator here on earth.

The Bitter Cry

After Jacob departed from the tent of his father, Esau entered with the dish he prepared for his father. Esau then learned that his brother had received the blessing. His response was unexpected:

> When Esau heard his father's words, he let out a most loud and bitter scream. "Bless me too, Father," he pleaded. Isaac said, "Your brother came with deceit, and he already took your blessing."
>
> – Genesis 27:34-35

The wail that issued from Esau's lips does not seem to be one of sorrow or self-pity but of loss. We might comprehend

---

[85] Nosson Slifkin, *Lying for the Truth* (Targum Press, Southfield, MI 1996) p. 84

the true nature of his response if we consider that he could just have easily screamed, "But you owe me, father!"

When it became apparent that he had not blessed Esau, Isaac was immediately seized with a fit of trembling. His reaction has resulted in a variety of opinions from the sages. Some commentaries teach that the trembling came from having finally grasped the true nature of Esau, coupled with the realization that Isaac had almost blessed the wrong son. In telling Esau that Jacob had already taken the blessing, Isaac is affirming his realization that it, indeed, belonged to his younger son. Esau's wrath was so intense that one has to ponder whether Isaac may have also felt that his eldest was capable of killing him in a fit of rage. Though he showed honor to his father and treated him with deference, it was respect, devoid of any affection. Esau believed he was due the same when he eventually became patriarch. His enthusiasm in preparing what his father thought was his final meal revealed in Esau the hope that Isaac had little time left to live. He couldn't wait to see him die.

The wail that issued from the lips of Esau resonates through the centuries.

> Isn't he truly named Jacob! He went behind my back twice. First he took my birthright, and now he took my blessing!
>
> – Genesis 27:36

The charges leveled against his brother are true. In spite of the fact that his cause was righteous, Jacob accomplished his goal through deception. However, Esau laced his complaint with an outright lie. Jacob acquired the birthright with the full consent of Esau who willingly bartered away his rights in exchange for some fast food.

PART TWO

WRESTLING WITH ANGELS

Chapter Eleven

THE MARRIAGE-GO-ROUND

> Isaac summoned Jacob and gave him a blessing and a charge. "Do not marry a Canaanite Girl," he said. "Set out and go to Padan Aram, to the house of your maternal grandfather Bethuel. Marry a daughter of your uncle Laban. God Almighty will then bless you, make you fruitful, and increase your numbers. You will become an assembly of nations. He will grant Abraham's blessing to you and your descendants, so that you will take over the land which God gave to Abraham, where you previously lived only as a foreigner." Isaac then sent Jacob on his way.
>
> – Genesis 28:1 - 28:5

Isaac had accepted, unreservedly, that the blessing and birthright belonged to Jacob. His acquiescence was emblematic of how the Patriarchs and Matriarchs recognized every event in their lives as the will of the Creator. Jacob exhibited this same level of trust in G-d by following his parent's wishes that he find a wife from the family of Laban – a man of particularly dubious character.

If we defer to the account found in *Sefer HaYashar*, which places the Torah narrative into a linear, chronological context, we discover that the above directive to Jacob from his father was actually spoken years after the blessing had been bestowed on him and he had already fled from the murderous wrath of Esau. Indeed, when Isaac repeated the blessing that we see above, Jacob had just returned, after 14 years in the house of Eber. It was actually his second extended visit. At the age of 18, Jacob and Esau had been invited to study with Eber and his remarkable father Shem, still very much alive at that time.[86] Jacob jumped at the prospect of learning in such a unique yeshiva but Esau declined.[87]

Esau moved far away to Mount Seir when Jacob sought the protection of Eber. It was around that time that Esau began to extend his family. In Genesis 26:34 we learn that Esau married Judith, daughter of Beeri and Basemath, daughter of Elon. Ten chapters later we notice what seems to be a contradiction:

> Esau took wives from the daughters of Canaan. These were Adah, daughter of Elon the Hittite, and Oholibamah, daughter of Anah, daughter of Tziv'on the Hivite. [He also married] Basemath, daughter of Ishmael [and] sister of Nebayoth. – Genesis 36:2-3

It would appear that he married two women who shared the same name. The Oral Tradition does offer some clarity on this issue:

> ....and Esau saw there a woman from among the daughters of Heth whose name was Bosmath, the daughter of Elon the Hittite, and he took her for a wife in addition to his first wife, and Esau called her name Adah, saying the blessing had in that time passed from him. – *Sefer HaYashar* 29:12

Obviously, Esau bestowed the new name on the Hittite woman to allay any confusion. Even though this detail is helpful, when one scans the lengthy genealogy of Esau in

---

86 The reader will recall that Shem, the son of Noah, was also known by the title of Melchizedek, who blessed Abraham.

87 *Sefer HaYashar* 28:17-18

Chapter 36 of Genesis, it can be a bit bewildering. There is a reason. As stated previously, the words of Torah are often transmitted in a manner that embodies the very essence of the event described. For example, the sale of the birthright is told with brevity because that's exactly how the transaction went down – no frills or fanfare. The method of describing the sale accurately conveys how Esau regarded the whole matter as a trifle. In the same way, the lineage of Esau is recorded so as to unmask the chaotic brew of messy family associations and blurred domestic lines. This was a dynasty rampant with incest. Esau and Adah produced a son they named Eliphaz. As we shall see, Eliphaz fathered a lineage that became Israel's worst enemy.

Chapter 28 of Genesis begins with an affirmation of Jacob's blessing and ends with Esau having a minor but misguided epiphany. When Isaac asked Jacob to refrain from any conjugal union with Canaanite women it occurred to Esau that his brother had been granted enormous favor by simply marrying into an approved family. Esau believed he could gain similar approval with a ruse – a tactic that might even move his father to revoke the sale of the birthright and allow him full benefit of the attendant blessings. Whatever his thinking, Esau married Machalat, from his Uncle Ishmael's family, yet he kept his rebellious idol worshipping Canaanite wives.[88] His serious lapse in judgment might be attributed to a negative trait acquired from his father: blindness. Esau was unable to see that it was his thoroughly corrupt character that had cost him the birthright – not his choice in wives. Failure to honestly see his own flaws, illustrated again, that Esau was unsuited to lead a holy nation.

[88] Hittites are descendants of Canaan; therefore the text also refers to these women as Canaanites.

Chapter Twelve

A DREAM OF KINGDOMS

According to Rashi, Jacob was 77 years old when he departed from Beersheva and headed north to Padan Aram to find a wife. As described in Genesis 28:5, Jacob bids his parent farewell and just five verses later he stops for the night. The reader might have the impression that Jacob's excursion was uneventful. But it was just the opposite. The Oral Torah paints a different picture. Jacob had just survived an ambush by a band of brigands led by his nephew, Eliphaz, the son of Esau. Eliphaz was only 13, but already a formidable hunter on par with Esau. It was his father who had dispatched him to intercept Jacob and kill him.

When Eliphaz eventually caught up with Jacob, he was prepared to put him to death but was so moved by Jacob's plea for mercy that he relented. Elizphaz knew that Esau would be furious when he heard that Jacob had been spared. Hoping to assuage his father's anger, he took all of Jacob's possessions, including his gold and silver, leaving his uncle in utter poverty.

The destitute Jacob found his way to Mount Moriah, the future location of *Beit HaMikdash* (Holy Temple). The description of the site is simply *HaMakom*, literally The Place. Throughout the Hebrew text of the Torah it is referenced in this manner. For example, in the commandment to only bring offerings to the Temple when it is established, the phrase *HaMakom* appears:

> This you may do only on the place that G-d your
>
> Lord will choose from among the tribes, as a

> dwelling established in His name. It is there that
>
> you shall go to seek his presence.
>
> – Deuteronomy 12:5

And what a place it is. Jacob beds down for the night falling into a state of deep REM sleep. He is treated to a propitious scene that opens with a magnificent ladder set upon the earth reaching to heavens and on it angels are ascending and descending. We know that this so-called ladder is quite distinctive because the Hebrew word employed is *sulom* and it is the only time the word is found in the entire Torah.

The dream is profound and richly layered. The interpretation can be unlocked by keeping in mind that the Torah is the blueprint for creation. We shall scrutinize the delicate symbolic strands of the ladder for a deeper understanding.

As a rule, when a plural is given in the Torah without a specific numerical designation, then the plural means two. There are *malakhim*, plural for angels both going up and down. Therefore, there are four angels in the dream. *Malakhim* simply means messengers. If we begin with the most elementary explanation of creation we know that there are four nucleotide bases found on the DNA strand – adenine, cytosine, guanine, thymine. These four provide the formation of all living matter and do so, *acting as messengers*.

Linguist Isaac Mozeson suggests that *sulom* is the Hebraic root for a word known to all Olympic skiers – slalom:

> SLALOM is a noun or verb of skiing in a zigzag, downhill race. The word is Norwegian; no Indo-European base or "root" is available. SLANT (also

> no Indo-European "root") is from Norwegian *slenta* (a slope), so that an SLN or SLM etymon of sloping up or down is needed.
>
> SOOLahM [Hebrew] is the ladder, ramp or stairway in Jacob's dream in Genesis 28:12.[89]

If we visualize someone speeding downhill through a slalom course, their tracks resemble a spiral.

To summarize:

- *Sulom* is the source of the Norwegian word slalom
- The double helix is a spiral, ladder-like structure
- Four angels move up and down on Jacob's Ladder as messengers
- Four nucleotide bases act as messengers on the DNA ladder

The *sulom* in the Torah is the spiraling DNA strand that connects heaven and earth.

There are a number of Biblical concepts that can be gleaned from Jacob's Ladder as a symbolic DNA strand. The double-helix coiling upwards from Mount Moriah to heaven recalls the creation of Adam from the dust of that very same site. The four angels can also be likened to the *kohanim* or priests ordained by the Creator at Mount Sinai just over 3,300 years ago.

The latest research has shown that significant numbers of

[89] Mozeson's *E-Word Dictionary*, a CD with a searchable database containing over 1,000 pages of words derived from Hebraic/Edenic roots (Lightcatcher Books, Springdale, AR)

Jewish males, many with Levitical surnames, carry a unique and specific genetic marker called the Cohen Modal Haplotype. The CMH is believed to have first appeared a little over 3,000 years ago, thus supporting the principle that the Aaronic priesthood was established and passed directly from fathers to sons, just over 3,300 years ago.[90]

> ...so that they will be priests to Me. It will be done so that their anointing will make them an eternal priesthood for all generations.
>
> – Exodus 40:15

There is yet another association between the hereditary priesthood, the heavenly ladder and Sinai. The reader may be familiar with *Gematria*, a method of interpretation made possible because Hebrew letter are also numbers. Mystical hints and even teachings can be derived by adding up the value of the letters in Hebrew words or phrases. For example, adding up all the letters in *elohim* – which can mean G-d or judges – yields the number 86. When the letters for *HaTeva*, meaning nature, are added, the sum is also 86. The fact that one of the titles for the G-d has the same *gematria* as the word for nature teaches us that G-d is creator of the material realm but also, as the Supreme Judge He created laws that control the physical world. Now consider the words *sulom* and Sinai, as well as the phrase *HaKohanim* (The Priests). They all have the same *gematria* of 130.[91] The relationship between Sinai, the priests and Jacob's Ladder should be obvious.

The most accessible meaning of the dream can be found in the very words spoken by G-d to Jacob. The creator unveils

---

[90] See Jacob Kleiman's *DNA & The Bible: The Genetic Link*. Springdale, AR: Lightcatcher Books, 2010

[91] Gutman G. Locks, *The Spice of Torah--Gematria* (Judaica Press, New York, 1985) p. 71

an expansive panorama of history, of Israel's relationship to the land and how, as a nation, they will be an instrument used by G-d to spread His goodness around the planet:

> I am God, Lord of Abraham your father, and Lord of Isaac. I will give to you and your descendants the land upon which you are lying. Your descendants will be like the dust of the earth. You shall spread out to the west, to the east, to the north, and to the south. All families on the earth will be blessed through you and your descendants.
>
> — Genesis 28:13-14

My teacher, the late Vendyl Jones, of blessed memory, would summon an image from his rural childhood days to demonstrate how the spiraled ladder imagery represented Israel's central role in the development of humanity. He likened the function of the Jewish nation to a farm implement called a grain augur. The device is used to draw grain from a truck into a barn. As the augur turns, it pulls the grain upward. As Vendyl would say, "Israel is the radial axis of history." The sages also saw the *sulom* in much the same way. Israel is literally at the center of all things. The spiraled shape also alludes to time and the cyclical nature of history as it revolves around the Jewish nation. Each angel represents one of the four world empires that will ascend to power and then descend. The analogy is very fitting since empires appear gradually on the world scene and in the same manner fall into decline.

Each rung represented a year. In his dream, Jacob watched as Babylon's angel climbed 70 rungs and descended. The angel of the Persian Empire went up 52 rungs then climbed back down. The angel of Greece was the next to ascend, going up 180 rungs of the ladder before descending. However, when the *malakh* of Edom scaled the ladder, Jacob was shaken to see that final angel climb *out of sight*. Jacob's fears are eased when HaShem tells him that Esau's influence as Edom would extend far into the future, but before he reaches the Throne of G-d, Esau/Edom will be cast down.[92] The prophet Obadiah also speaks of Edom's fate:

> The pride of thy heart hath beguiled thee, O thou that dwelt in the clefts of the rock, thy habitation on high; that say in thy heart: 'Who shall bring me down to the ground?' Though thou make thy nest as high as the eagle, and though thou set it among the stars, I will bring thee down from thence, saith the LORD.
>
> – Obadiah 1:3 - 4

Even though Jacob's descendants, the Jewish People, are central to history, the dream of Jacob also reveals the influence of the four empires over Israel – even until the latter days. Most readers will recognize this imagery in another source – the Book of Daniel. His writings portrayed Babylon, Persia, Greece and Rome as prophetic emblems in the dreams of Nebuchadnezzar. Those nations figured profoundly in the landscape of the Jewish experience, but we might wonder why Egypt and Assyria are missing from these visions. The answer can be found in the placement of the ladder in the dream.

The four angels who represent the four world empires travel up and down a ladder that is set upon the Temple Mount. This aspect alone sets the Big Four apart from Egypt and Assyria. Though the rulers of these two kingdoms could boast that they held sway over the Jewish people and their land, even exacting tribute from the treasuries of the Temple, but they differ from the four empires of Daniel in

[92] *Perkei Rabbi Eliezer*, p. 265

one major respect: they never controlled or destroyed the Temple. The ascendancy of Babylon, Persia, Greece and Rome is marked by their control of Israel's holiest site.

One more reason those empires loom so profoundly is that their cumulative influence is still with us today embodied in the last *malakh* to climb the ladder: the angel of Edom. The idea of obscuring the time of Edom's descent can be found in the Book of Daniel when the prophet is told to "seal up the book."

> Jacob awoke from his sleep. "God is truly in this place," he said, "but I did not know it." He was frightened. "How awe-inspiring this place is!" he exclaimed. "It must be God's temple. It is the gate to heaven!"
>
> — Genesis 28:16-17

Jacob's reaction is appropriate for the monumental vision that the dream offered. Rashi tells us that if Jacob had realized the holiness of the site, he never would have made his bed there for the night. He felt so strongly about the experience that he was compelled to round up stones, set them in place and pour oil on them, marking the place --- there's that phrase again, *HaMakom* – as the future site of the *Beit HaMikdash*, the Holy Temple. The remarkable spot is known as the Gate of Heaven and for good reason. It was also the location of the *Even Shetyiah*, the Foundation Stone that was part of the bedrock that served as a massive keystone, its other end sunk into the depths of the earth. The formation is said to be secured firmly to the very center of the planet. When the Holy Temple was eventually built, the stone was located inside the Holy of Holies with the Ark of the Covenant resting upon it.

Revived and fortified with the promises of the Creator, Jacob made his way to Padan Aram where he was forced to deal with the artful trickster, Laban, so that he could marry the lovely Rachel. Laban believed the bad press about Jacob and felt no compunction in dealing with a man he viewed as an even bigger con artist than him. Through deceit, he forced Jacob into a marriage with Rachel's older sister Leah. Jacob eventually married Rachel. Thanks to his G-d-given genius and hard work he became wealthy.

After 25 years, he gathered up his extended family and his riches to leave Padan Aram and establish a home. The Torah details the displeasure of Laban when he learned that the entire brood had made a hasty getaway. He chased them, knowing he has just lost his meal ticket. Their relationship was the first fulfillment of the promise that G-d would bless those who blessed Jacob but curse those that cursed him.

Jacob had prospered – yet Laban, jealous of his success, attempted to swindle him time after time – even appropriating the inheritance of his own daughters. Seeing his treachery, the women made it clear that they were on board with leaving their father:

> Rachel and Leah both spoke up. "Do we then still have a portion and an inheritance in our father's estate?" they exclaimed. "Why, he treats us like strangers! He has sold us and spent the money! All the wealth that God has taken from our father actually belongs to us and our children. Now, whatever God has said to you, do it!"
>
> – Genesis 31:14 - 16

When Laban caught up with Jacob and company, he portrayed himself as the victim, that he had been shabbily treated by his son-in-law. Jacob responded, in his defense, that the reason their exodus was conducted in haste and without warning, was to avoid the possibility of a dangerous confrontation.

Finally, Jacob only appeased his father-in-law when he agreed to a provision that he never mistreat Laban's daughters. They sealed the pact with a meal and a heap of stones to mark the occasion.

The spare language of the English translations of the Torah might lead us to believe that Laban had honored the spirit of the agreement. The sages tell us that Laban was only sincere at the moment that he made the pact. The Torah states that the next day, *"Laban returned to his place."* The verse can be understood in the sense that Laban reverted to his devious ways. According to the Oral Tradition, he sent word via a small party of men to alert Esau what had transpired. The message was a concoction of half-truths compounded by blatant lies in which he complained that after enjoying his generous hospitality, Jacob had deceived him, stolen his property and taken his daughters by force.

The reader will note the order in which these things were listed by Laban – his daughters came last. Laban epitomized "those who would curse Jacob" throughout the ages. Lastly, Laban informed Esau exactly where he could find Jacob.[93] That would explain why Jacob, in the very next chapter of the Torah, sent lengthy dispatches to Esau with pleas that he be allowed to continue his journey in peace.

Fueled by his brand of self-righteous indignation, Esau gathers a force of armed men intent on intercepting his brother. The Torah details the preparations made by Jacob as he anticipated a volatile reunion. Before their fateful meeting, Jacob has another experience that presages the history of his descendants. He arrived at the Jabbok River, about to wade across. Once again, we see the patriarchal and prophetic template evoked. Abraham was called the *Ivri* which denotes "one who crosses over" because he had done

[93] *Sefer HaYashar* 31:54

so at the Euphrates. It was an act that symbolized his departure from an outmoded philosophy to a new way of thinking and living. And Jacob was doing the same. Before he could, Jacob had to wrestle with a man until dawn.

Face Time

In one of the most celebrated wrestling bouts in history, Jacob is almost defeated by a man described by Rashi as the angel of Esau. There are countless meanings that we can extract from this imagery and they all apply and are equally important. If we look at the name that Jacob gave to the site of this wrestling match we can begin to understand just how grand this experience was. Jacob called the site Peniel, exclaiming:

> I have seen Elohim face to face but my life was
>
> saved!
>
> — Genesis 32:31

Indeed, the name reflects a major revelation for Jacob. After surviving what was either a genuine tumble in the dirt with a flesh and blood adversary or a turbulent and deeply personal dark night of the soul, Jacob finally understood that no matter what he encountered in life — whether man or angel, good or evil, whatever the trial or experience — everything was placed before him by the G-d of his forefathers.

In describing the "face" of G-d, he also expressed his profound joy at being part of the whole glorious, wonderful, fearful rewarding experience that we call life. Most importantly, he also saw the span of history and his own place in it. Yes, in that *Face* he had seen the whole reason for his existence. Is it any wonder that, of all the patriarchs, he was the one who dreamed of the ladder connecting heaven and earth? It was he and his offspring who would bring the two together.

After his all-night struggle, Jacob was called Israel, a multi-faceted designation that can be rendered either "upright with G-d" or "man struggling with G-d." More than a name, *Israel* is really a noble and prophetic title that reveals how the plan of the Creator would be implemented in the material world. It was to be borne by the one who fully realized that ever since creation, G-d desired a true partnership in building the world. After Adam, that partnership would require a genuine struggle to achieve heaven on earth. That holy struggle was part of Jacob's epiphany and he was the first to fully realize that holy task and accept it.

His wrestling partner also gave Jacob something else – an injury that caused him to limp for the remainder of his life. The wound, inflicted on the inner thigh (near his reproductive organs) is a hint that the descendants of Esau would come perilously close to destroying the descendants of Jacob.

On another level, that injury may also be symbolic of the angel locating a congenital flaw in the body of Jacob, symbolic of the kindness of the Jewish people. Possibly we can trace that weakness found in the patriarch Abraham. It was his insistence on showing too much kindness to his enemies. The wrestling exposed that tiny flaw and from that moment on, Israel has been limping to the finish line of history, held back from fulfilling their ultimate destiny—a characteristic that continues to weaken the modern state of Israel.

Esau is Edom

Israel is a title that could have been bestowed on Esau had he not rejected the Divine plan. Instead, Esau became known as Edom, which is "red." This ignoble name hints at his desire for domination of Jacob's descendants, as well as the rest of the world through bloody warfare. The name Edom is taken from the root, *adom* – the dirt that he chose to wallow in because of his blatant disregard for everything sacred. It expresses his earthbound humanist philosophy that only man has all the answers and need not look to heaven for guidance.

The words of Hashem to Rebecca reveal these aspects of her twins. The lives of the brothers would provide the template for distinct national character traits. Jacob, as Israel, embodied his people's striving for a higher purpose; to rebuild the world based on Torah. Jacob looked to the Creator for direction in all things. Esau rejected the G-d of his father in favor of the most alluring idol of all – himself. That god is still expressed in the man-made ideologies held so dearly by the Western world today. The offspring of both brothers would worship, procreate, build, govern and war as they lived – according to these opposing concepts.

The Edomite kings ruled before Israel ever crowned a king. The historical precedence enjoyed by Esau is embedded in the events following the struggle with the angel at Penuel. After he departs from that site, Jacob has a fateful reunion with Esau and four hundred of his men. Their conversation is an example of a prophetic plan being unveiled within a seemingly mundane exchange of words. Esau urges his brother to join his company and they will travel to the home of Esau in Mount Seir. But Jacob demurs:

> Please go ahead of me, my lord. I will lead my group slowly, following the pace of the work that I

> have ahead of me, and the pace of the children. I
>
> will eventually come to [you], my lord, in Seir.
>
> – Genesis 33:14

Indeed, Esau did 'go ahead' of Jacob. History is a witness of these words coming to pass. Esau, as Edom – the embodiment of the Western world, established a foothold with the Greco-Roman culture and continues to influence our lives today. However, as vividly promised by the prophets, the Jewish People as Israel will one day take their rightful place at the head of the nations.[94]

The dominance of Esau and his offspring is also revealed in the royal list of Edom in Chapter 36 of Genesis. One entry found in that same chapter's survey of Edomite clans is Magdiel, which according to Rabbi Eliezer, is the Roman Empire:[95]

> The Rambam and Ibn Ezra are unequivocal in maintaining that Edom symbolized the Roman Empire.[96]

While there is consensus that Edom is Rome, the various sages differ on some of the specifics. For instance, Rashi held that the aforementioned Magdiel represents Rome, while the Rambam disagreed. In Midrash Rabbah on Genesis 36:42, the Roman emperor Diocletian is compared to Magdiel. In Chapter Fifteen, we will investigate this prophetic connection.

---

[94] Obadiah 1:21, Jeremiah 29:14, Amos 9:14

[95] *Perkei Rabbi Eliezer,*. p. 290, also see Midrash Rabbah on Genesis 36:43

[96] Book of Daniel, *The Artscroll Tanach* (Mesorah, NY) p. 105

The people of Edom would, at times, appoint men from other nations as their rulers. This is true of Bela, son of Beor, who is said to be from the lineage of Laban and ancestor of the infamous sorcerer Balaam. Genesis 36:32 states that Bela, relocated his throne to Dinhabah, a locale that figures prominently in this saga. Another scourge of Israel was the *mamzer* known as Amalek. His unending murderous campaign has been waged in what military historians might term the Middle Eastern Theater of conflict. But Amalek had a half-brother who troubled Israel while the Twelve Tribes were still in Egypt enjoying relative freedom. This half-brother eventually spread his dominance into Europe. His name was Zepho:

> These are the names of Esau's sons: Eliphaz the son of Adah the wife of Esau, Reuel the son of Basemath of Esau. The sons of Eliphaz were Teman, Omar, Zepho, Gatam, and Kenaz. (Timna was a concubine of Eliphaz, Esau's son; she bore Amalek to Eliphaz.)
>
> — Genesis 36:11[97]

This little-known figure from antiquity is the vital link that connects Edom to Rome.

> Thus saith the LORD; For three transgressions of Edom, and for four, I will not turn away the punishment thereof; because he did pursue his brother with the sword, and did cast off all pity, and his anger did tear perpetually, and he kept his wrath forever.
>
> — Amos 1:11

Amalek, a prince of Edom, revealed his bitter roots by exhibiting the basest values and employing violence to achieve

[97] He is also listed among the Chiefs of Edom in Genesis 36:15.

dominance over Israel. Zepho, his half-brother, was just as cunning, if not more so. Derived from the Hebrew root for *secret*, his name also denotes a spy. Their grandfather, Esau, taught both of them that one could ensnare others with guile.[98]

However, if words failed, then one should resort to the sword.

Zepho's conflict with the Children of Israel is key to uncovering the long-buried but crucial geographic, historic and cultural signposts that lead directly back to the founding of ancient Rome. We can follow the influence of that empire's Greco-Roman principles that still exert an influence on the thinking in much of the Western world today. Popular historian Michael Grant describes the pervasiveness of that influence :

> We ourselves, whether we like it or not, are the heirs of the Greeks and the Romans. In a thousand different ways, they are permanently and indestructibly woven into the fabric of our own existence.[99]

We will now journey through forgotten history. We will discover how the infamous Zepho plays a pivotal role in precipitating the harsh bondage of the Exodus, his

[98] Genesis 25:28 can also be rendered that Esau was "a trapper with his mouth" - see *The Living Torah* by Rabbi Aryeh Kaplan (Mozanim Publishers, 1989) p. 116

[99] Grant, *The Founders of the Western World* (Scribner, New York, 1991) p. 1

connection to a hero who survived the fall of Troy and his travels to the coasts of Africa and Biblical *Kittim*. Before we determine Zepho's impact we need to set the stage – to locate the geographical pieces of the puzzle that will come together before he arrives on the scene.

> When the most High divided to the nations their inheritance, when He separated the sons of Adam, He set the bounds of the people according to the number of the children of Israel.
>
> – Deuteronomy 32:8

The nations of the world were divided into 70 distinct cultures and tongues. The number of souls who immigrated to Egypt with the patriarch Jacob determined the separation. These words are also linked to the scattering of mankind after the destruction of the Tower of Babel. The *Zohar* (I, 177a) reveals that each nation was put under the authority of an angel.

Where did each angel lead those nations?

There is no specific reference to a nation named Rome in the *Tanach*. The Roman armies did not reach the shores of Israel until well after the termination of the Prophetic Era. The last of the prophets, Ezra and Nehemiah passed away in the Jewish year 3448 (312 BCE) and that same year also marked the beginning of Greek domination of the Jewish people.[100] Rome would not impact Israel for at least another 200 years.

It would take a people fueled by ruthless ambition to found an empire like Rome. That is why the Jewish commentators identify Rome with Edom. They possessed the DNA of Esau. It drove them to become a people known for the forceful

---

[100] Rabbi Shlomo Rotenberg, *Am Olam: History of the Eternal Nation*, (Keren Pub., Brooklyn, NY) p. 71

and brutal manner in which they seized the world stage.

The founder of Rome was said to have been Romulus. He and his twin, Remus, were descendants of Aeneas who departed his homeland following the fall of Troy. He made his way to Macedonia, then the island of Sicily and eventually to the Italian Peninsula. According to Livy, Aeneas founded a dynasty and his descendants ruled in the region until the time of Armulius, who seized power by murdering the rightful male heir to the throne. Armulius spared Rhea, the surviving daughter, but banished her into service as a Vestal Virgin to insure that she had no royal issue. The virgin miraculously became pregnant – claiming she had relations with the god Mars and gave birth to twins. They were promptly thrown into the River Tiber. The boys were spared when they floated along the banks and were caught in the low branches of a fig tree and found by a she-wolf. The creature suckled them until they were discovered by a shepherd. When the boys became adults, they learned of their royal lineage and set out to build a nation. In one account, Remus was killed in a dispute with Romulus who then established the city of Rome on seven hills. [101]

Rome's early history is really the province of poets which is one reason it is so difficult to find hard evidence of its beginnings. On the other hand, the Talmud, *Sefer HaYashar*, *Seder HaOlam* and other sources offer clues to the origin of this empire and its ultimate influence on Israel.

The Upright Book

Sefer HaYashar takes the reader back to the very early development of Rome and presents surprising parallels to aforementioned Aeneas and his journey from Troy to Italy.

If you will indulge me, I feel it necessary to digress for the

[101] Aubrey De Selincourt, *Livy: Early History of Rome* (Penguin Classics, Middlesex, UK, 1960) pp. 35-40

sake of the reader unfamiliar with *Sefer HaYashar*. The Hebrew title of this work is often rendered as "Book of Jasher" in most English translations of the Bible. Endorsements for the book are found in Joshua 10:13 and 2 Samuel 1:18. The reference in Joshua is from the miraculous event of the sun standing still during Israel's battle against the Amorites in the Valley of Ayalon and rhetorically asks, "Is this not written in the Book of Jasher?"

Avraham Davis, of Yosher Press and editor of the most recent English edition, maintains that the origins of the work are uncertain, yet it has been quoted by Jewish scholars for ages. *Sefer HaYashar* is referenced throughout the exhaustive commentary known as *Me'Am Loez*, compiled nearly 250 years ago by the great Sephardic sage Rabbi Yaakov Culi.[102]

First printed in Naples in 1553, the language of *Sefer HaYashar* reflects a grasp of geography that is definitely post-Biblical. Locales such as Lombardy and Tuscany are mentioned.

The English-language translation of *Sefer HaYashar* was first published in America in 1840. The title, *Book of Jasher*, confuses those unfamiliar with Hebrew and they construe the title as an author's name. Of course, Jasher is the anglicized rendering of the Hebrew *yashar* which means straight or upright. The title literally means "Upright Book." Some hold that the title refers to the book's source, the Torah – the ultimate upright book. Others believe the *yashar* of the title is indicative of the book's placing the events of the Torah in chronological order.

The Jewish scholar responsible for the 1840 English

---

102 The English translation of *MeAm Loez* comes to us through the efforts of the late Rabbi Aryeh Kaplan, of blessed memory.

translation of *Sefer HaYashar* was Mordechai Manuel Noah, an extraordinary journalist and diplomat who rubbed shoulders with the likes of John Adams and Stephen Decatur. He was also American's first consul to the Middle East. Though Noah did much to promote the cause of Jews in America, he also believed in the return of the Jewish people to the Holy Land. An entire book could be devoted to the achievements of this remarkable gentleman.

His translation is still with us today. It is public domain and available from a variety of publishers, including the author's own company. We decided to publish author Wayne Simpson's version, *The Authentic Annals of the Early Hebrews*, because Mr. Simpson provides the 1840 translation intact, as well as a lengthy history of the *Sefer HaYashar's* origins.

Chapter Thirteen

THE VEIL OF HISTORY

> The sons of Javan were Elishah, Tarshish, Kittim, and Dodanim.
>
> – Genesis 10:4

Previously, we dealt with the destruction of the Tower of Babel and the dispersion that followed. The Tower fell the same year that Peleg, son of Eber died, suggesting that the calamity was caused by the splitting of the earth's continents.[103] It further alludes to the dispersion of the survivors across the globe. According to the Jewish chronology this massive seismic event occurred 1,996 years from Adam or around 1764 BCE.[104]

The Jewish historian, Flavius Josephus, confirmed that Javan was the ancestor of the Greeks.[105] It is in the Torah's catalog of new nations that we see a future affinity between the Greek and Romans. Noah's son, Japheth, was the father of Javan. Genesis adds a very helpful geographic note:

> By these were the isles of the Gentiles divided in their lands; every one after his tongue, after their families, in their nations." [106]

Javan is then the ancestor whose descendants founded a group of cities of coastal Asia Minor and nearby islands that became known as Ionia. Javan is easily converted to Ion. In

---

[103] cf. Genesis 10:25, "for in his (Peleg's) days the earth was divided."

[104] *Am Olam*, p. 39

[105] Chapter 6, *Antiquities of the Jews*, trans. by Wm. Whiston, p. 31

[106] Genesis 10:1-4

the Hebrew text Javan is spelled with a *yud* which can be transposed to an "i" while the aleph remains silent. The *vav* can be pronounced with a long "o" sound and the letter *nun* remains an "n" sound. This gives us Ion. Chapter 10:15, *Sefer HaYashar* is helpful in our search for the Javan/Ion connection to Italy:

> ...the children of Elisha (son of Javan,) are the Almanim, and they built themselves cities...and of them were the people of Lumbardi, who dwell between the mountains of Job and Shbathmo, and they conquered the land of Italia.

This is consistent with the concept that those who first settled the mountainous northern area of Italy were directly related to the Ionian Greeks. This surely is the source for Greece's other name of Ellas or Hellas from which we derive the term for Greek religious concepts known as Hellenism. The name Ellas may also be the source for the Grecian heavenly realm called the Elysian Fields.

The next verse reveals even more detail – "And the children of Kittim are the Romin who dwell in the valley of Canopia by the river Tiberu."

Rome was founded on the banks of the River Tiber. The Aramaic text known as the *Targum* also identifies *Kittim* as Italy.[107]

Even though the Torah lists the immediate offspring of Javan, there seems to be no consensus among the great rabbinic

---

[107] *Living Torah,* footnote on p. 40

commentators regarding the secular historic identities of the nations they founded. This is especially true of the people known as the Kittim. Some offer that the latter were the first to settle the isle of Cyprus; others say that they are the Greeks, while various commentators suggest that the Kittim are the Romans. I believe that they are all correct.

Everything about the Kittim indicates that they represent a people who spread, in an incremental fashion. Beginning at Cyprus, we can see the ruins of Citium that have been dated to around the 13th Century BCE. It seems logical that these people continued their westward expansion by colonizing what became Greece and eventually moved into the Italian Peninsula. Flavius Josephus supports this view by stating that Kittim was the collective name given to the populace of all the islands and to most of the countries near the sea. [108]

The late Hanan Eshel, an Israeli archaeologist and Dead Sea Scrolls scholar, remarked that the Kittim are mentioned in seven of the Dead Sea Scrolls and that their reference in the scrolls was, "clearly related to the imperialism of Rome."[109]

Mainstream historians consider the Bible the stuff of legend, yet the origins of Greece and Rome are mythological. The accounts come down to us from the likes of Herodotus, Eusebius and Titus Livius who all default to mythological sources. The Greeks and Romans share something in common with most ancient cultures – shoddy record-keeping. They cannot decisively pinpoint their own national origins. In his *The Early History of Rome*, Titus Livius admits that the task of writing of Rome's beginning is hampered by a lack of hard information but, frankly, this is of little concern to him:

---

108 *Antiquites of the Jews*, Book One, 6:1

109 Hanan Eshel, *"The Kittim in the War Scroll and in the Pesharim"* (Orion Center for the Dead Sea Scrolls and Associated Literature, 1999)

> Events before the birth of Rome have come to us in old tales with more of the charm of poetry than of a sound historical record, and such traditions I propose neither to affirm or refute.[110]

He goes on to lament that the typical reader of his day might find tales of high antiquity just plain boring. Centuries later, Sir Isaac Newton tackled the issue of murky historic timetables in his *Chronology of the Ancient Kingdoms Amended*. Newton drew from several classical Greek sources to illustrate the problems with the generally accepted origins of the Greeks. In the introduction to his book, Newton made a serious charge, that "*they have made the Antiquities of Greece three or four hundred years older than the truth.*" In subsequent chapters, he related the same difficulty with dates for the founding of Rome:

> And as for the Chronology of the Latines, that is still more uncertain. Plutarch represents great uncertainties in the Originals of Rome: and so doth Servius. The old records of the Latines were burnt by the Gauls, sixty and four years before the death of Alexander the great; and Quintus Fabius Pictor, the oldest historian of the Latines, lived an hundred years later

---

[110] Livy: *Early History of Rome*, p. 33

than that King.[111]

Most ancient cultures had little interest and were often oblivious to the significance of events that unfolded before their arrival. This chronological apathy infected cultures from the top down. Rulers were only interested in one kind of record – one which celebrated their own achievements. On the other hand, time has always been sacred to the Jews.

This holy aspect of time is even more evident in the numerous *mitzvoth* (commandments) given to Israel to commemorate appointed annual feasts. Israel was to be especially mindful of honoring the Sabbath, the seventh day of the week. Not only was this a primary commandment for Israel, their inescapable national destiny is tied to their faithful observance of *Shabbat*. Read the warnings of the prophet Nehemiah to the men of Judah:

> Then I contended with the nobles of Judah, and said unto them, "What evil thing is this that ye do, and profane the sabbath day? Did not your fathers thus, and did not our God bring all this evil upon us, and upon this city? Yet ye bring more wrath upon Israel by profaning the sabbath."
>
> – Nehemiah 13:17[112]

It is clear that the very of existence of the nation of Israel hinges on their observance of time as it affected the laws

[111] Isaac Newton, *The Chronology of Ancient Kingdoms, Amended, To which is Prefix'd, A Short Chronicle from the First Memory of Things in Europe, to the Conquest of Persia by Alexander the Great*, First published in 1728 by J. Tonsan and T. Longman, the text is now available from Kessinger Publishing, LLC (March 5, 2004) p. 49

[112] See Jeremiah 17:19

given at Sinai.[113] This determination to maintain a chronology is further illustrated in the Torah's numerous genealogies. While it is generally accepted that Rome was probably founded somewhere around 700 - 800 BCE, any observant Jew can tell you the exact date that the Torah was given – the 6th of Sivan, in the year 2448 (1312 BCE).[114] Since the Torah is, in reality, Israel's Constitution and Declaration of Independence, 6th Sivan, 2448, can be likened to our own July 4th. Israel is unique among the ancient nations in that it can trace its very beginning to an exact date over 3,300 years ago?[115]

Language can offer us some clues in our search for the roots of Greece and Rome. There is some difficulty since the Greeks Hellenized the identity of persons and places which can sometimes obscure their origin. This state of affairs is nothing new. Flavius Josephus encountered this same situation. In chapter five of his *Antiquities of the Jews* he wrote of the impact of the Greeks and expresses his comments in the form of a complaint:

> There were some also who passed over the sea in ships, and inhabited the islands; and some of those nations do retain their names which were given to them by their founders; but some have lost them also; and some have admitted certain changes in them that they might be more intelligible to the inhabitants; and they were the Greeks who became the authors of such

---

113 Rafael Eisenberg, *Survival: Israel & Mankind* (Feldheim, Jerusalem/NY, 1991) p.12

114 Eliezer Shulman, *Sequence of Events in the Old Testament* (Ministry of Defense Pbls. Tel-Aviv) p. 53

115 According to Cato, Rome was founded on the, *"11th of the Calends of May, in the first year of the 7th Olympiad,"* about 751 B.C.

> mutations, for when in after ages they became potent, they claimed to themselves the glory of antiquity-giving names to the nations that sounded well in Greek....as if they were a people derived from themselves.[116]

This Greek influence has, for example, tainted the study of ancient Egypt. We still reference many of the pharaohs by the Greek variant of their names. Today, we only know the monumental structures of ancient Egypt by the words bestowed on them by early Greek tourists. The most blatant examples seem to betray an Epicurean preoccupation because the word *pyramid* is actually what the Greeks called a wheat cake. The pointed stone monuments known today as *obelisks* are derived from the Greek word for a spit used to roast meat.[117]

Returning to the works of Josephus, the historian relates how these sons of Javan spread rapidly after the Tower and influenced much of the world in their time. The Romans borrowed heavily from the Greeks. On that point there is no dispute. The origins of Rome are intertwined with that of Greece.

Historian, R. M. Ogilvie, in his introduction to *The Early History of Rome,* relates that the nation's beginnings were not recorded until almost 300 years after its first kings ruled. Upon close examination it seems that these so-called early historical accounts of Rome were often *"Greek stories clothed in Roman dress."* [118]

Greece influenced the fledging Roman culture so much that

---

[116] *The Complete Works of Flavius Josephus* (Kregel Publications, Grand Rapids, MI, 1960) p. 30

[117] Alan Gardiner, *Egypt of the Pharaohs* (Oxford University Press, 1961) p. 2

[118] Livy: *Early History of Rome* , pp. 12-13

the southern region of Italy was once known as *Magna Graecia or* greater Greece. Italians were proud of the fact that the one could find more Greek ruins in Italy than in Greece.[119]

Perhaps the reason for this situation is more straightforward than we might first imagine. These influences are based on the fact that these nations simply shared the same ancestry. The common roots of the Romans and the Greeks can be gleaned from the Genesis account of Noah and his sons after the Flood. Since the Children of Israel have kept a record of their history through the nation's seminal events, we should be able to trace the origins of other nations who came in contact with Israel.

How did the country in which Rome was located come to be known as Italy? According to Dionysius of Halicarnassus, a contemporary of Livy, the name was derived from Italus, an ancient king who ruled the southernmost part of the peninsula. The region was originally settled by a Greek people called Oenotrians and that, "in the course of time Italus came to be their king, after whom they were named Italians."[120] Italus may have been named after the well-known mythological figure of Atlas, famous for carrying the earth on his shoulders. Dionysius also quotes other historians of his time and suggests that the colony we now call Rome developed gradually:

> ...there were two settlements of Rome, one a little
>
> after the Trojan war, and the other fifteen

---

[119]Peter D. Arnott, *The Romans and Their World* (St. Martins Press, NY,1970) p. 41

[120]*Dionysius of Halicarnassus: Roman Antiquities, Volume I, Books 1-2,* Translated by Earnest Cary (Loeb Classical Library, Cambridge, Mass. 1937) p.141

generations after the first. And if anyone desires to look into the remoter past, even a third Rome will be found, more ancient than these, one that was founded before Aeneas and the Trojans came into Italy. This is related by no ordinary or modern historian, but by Antiochus of Syracuse, whom I have mentioned before. He says that when Morges reigned in Italy (which at that time comprehended all the seacoast from Tarentum to Posidonia),a man came to him who had been banished from Rome. His words are these: "When Italus was growing old, Morges reigned. In his reign there came a man who had been banished from Rome; his name was Seicelus." According to the Syracusan historian, therefore, an ancient Rome is found even earlier than the Trojan war.[121]

Rape of the Sabine Women

When Rome became a world power, they deployed their naval fleets in their plan for conquest. This is further

[121]*Dionysius of Halicarnassus: Roman Antiquities, Volume I, Books 1-2,* Translated by Earnest Cary (Loeb Classical Library, Cambridge, Mass. 1937) p.245

developed in the Biblical references to the ships of *Kittim*.[122] Of course the prizewinner for Biblical references to ships is *Tarshish*, but we will deal with them in an upcoming chapter.

Let us look to another offspring of Japheth -- Tubal. He and his descendants also reveal an ethnic and historical link to the people of the Italian Peninsula. Tubal is found in Ezekiel 38 and Isaiah 66:

> And I will set a sign among them, and I will send those that escape of them unto the nations, to Tarshish, Pul, and Lud, that draw the bow; to Tubal, and Javan, to the isles afar off, that have not heard my fame, neither have seen my glory; and they shall declare my glory among the Gentiles.
>
> – Isaiah 66:19

Apparently, *Tubal* was located among the so-called island nations. *Sefer HaYashar* pinpoints the actual region by revealing that the sons of *Tubal* settled in *Tuscanuh*, near the Tiber, after making war against the children of *Kittim*. Afterwards the people of *Tubal* founded a city called *Sabinah*. This area is still easy to locate on modern maps north of Rome. It is a mountainous region with scattered marshes along its coasts.

Modern Tuscany also skirts an area once known as Sabine. It is here that the Jewish Oral Tradition recounts an episode that is nearly identical to the legends of ancient Rome.

According to Chapter 17 of *Sefer HaYashar*, the sons of Tubal suffered a massive defeat after an unprovoked assault by the warring Kittim. In the aftermath, the people of Tubal swore that they would never allow intermarriage between

---

122 Numbers 24:24; Daniel 11:30

Kittim and Tubal. This was too much for the lust-crazed men of Kittim because the daughters of Tubal were renowned for their beauty.

A delegation of ten men, sent to request wives, was rejected. The men of Kittim decided to take matters into their own hands. Three years later at harvest time, while the men of Tubal were away tending flocks in the fields, the men of Kittim kidnapped the women of Sabinah.[123] This act precipitated yet another war. A series of skirmishes ensued for a year. During one decisive battle, the Kittim realized they were about to face defeat and death, so they placed their sons and daughters on the battlements – exposing them to the onslaught of Tubal's warriors. The men of Kittim called down to the soldiers of Tubal that the youngsters were the offspring of the captured women of Sabinah in Tubal. It was obvious to the men of Tubal that they would lose their own daughters and grandchildren if they continued. Like it or not, the Kittim were their kinsmen. The warriors of Tubal returned to their homes in peace.

Now compare this with the account from Roman historian Titus Livius. He relates that during the time of Romulus, the mythical founder of Rome, there proved to be a shortage of wives for Roman men due to a ban imposed by neighboring villages against marrying Romans. Romulus at first sent an appeal to these settlements to please consider intermarriage. When his overtures were rebuffed, Romulus hatched a plot. He invited all the neighboring villages to an annual festival for Neptune. The people crowded into the city and among them, Livius notes, "...are all the Sabines."

While the throng was wrapped up in the excitement of the feast, a signal was given and the young Roman males ran into the crowd and carried off the Sabine woman of their

[123] *Sefer HaYashar, Chapter 17*

choice. Naturally a war ensued, with the attack being led by Tatius, king of the Sabines. The bloody conflict eventually came to an end when the kidnapped women of Sabine rushed to the front and divided both armies on the battlefield. The women bravely reminded both sides that despite the circumstances that made them brides – many of whom are now mothers – they are all related to the men on both sides. The effect was immediate. The leaders of Sabine and Rome forged a peace treaty and united the two states under one banner with Rome as the seat of power.[124]

This incident is also recalled in the plays of Gnaeus Naevius and Quintus Ennius. As recorded by Livy, this oft-told tale is generally characterized as legendary. Since it is has never been documented, the exact timeframe cannot be determined. But *Sefer HaYashar* records the same episode as history. It even marks the clash between these warring peoples as taking place in the same year that the patriarch Abraham turned ninety-one.

Legend claims that Romulus held the powerful Sabine-Roman alliance together for forty peaceful years until his literal departure from the earth – an event that convinced his followers of his heavenly origins. Livy relates that Romulus disappeared from sight while reviewing troops on the plains near Lake Capra. A violent storm arose, shrouding the proceedings in turbulent rains. When the raging torrent ceased as quickly as it had begun and the mist cleared, the throne of Romulus was empty. Though many believed Romulus had been taken to heaven, others suspected foul play. The rampant speculation was in danger of splitting the young nation apart when a certain Proculus Julius forestalled a revolt by reporting to the assembly:

> Romans, Romulus, the father of this city, suddenly descending from heaven, appeared to me this day

---

[124] *Livy: Early History of Rome* , pp. 43-48

> at day-break. While I stood covered with awe, and filled with a religious dread, beseeching him to allow me to see him face to face, he said, Go tell the Romans, that the gods so will, that my Rome should become the capitol of the world. Therefore let them cultivate the art of war, and let them know and hand down to posterity, that no human power shall be able to withstand the Roman arms. Having said this, he ascended up to heaven.

I think it quite remarkable that, in this fabled reportage of Rome's beginnings, that Romulus, an alleged demi-god, does not speak of elevating mankind but instead, reinforces the idea that the whole character and mission of the Roman people was to wage war and conquer the world.

In the fall of 2007, a team of Italian archaeologists unearthed a sanctuary they believed yielded the physical evidence of Rome's beginnings. The find included artifacts dating to the time of a ruler known as Numa Pompilius who was described as being a member of the Sabine tribe. At the age of 40, he succeeded Romulus on the throne but not before first rejecting kingship. The words of Numa, as reported by Plutarch, reveal how, at its very foundations, Rome was predisposed to war and conquest:

> Yet Romulus had the advantage to be thought divinely born and miraculously preserved and nurtured. My birth was mortal; I was reared and instructed by men that are known to you. The very points of my character that are most commended mark me as unfit to reign, -- love of retirement and of studies inconsistent with business, a passion that has become inveterate in me for peace, for unwarlike occupations, and for the society of men whose meetings are but those

> of worship and of kindly intercourse, whose lives in general are spent upon their farms and their pastures. I should but be, methinks, a laughing-stock, while I should go about to inculcate the worship of the gods, and give lessons in the love of justice and the abhorrence of violence and war, to a city whose needs are rather for a captain than for a king.

Numa believed he was unfit to lead because he was not a soldier. Nor did he share the philosophy of his predecessor – which was to conduct wars. The reign of Numa was marked by peace and he became known for his wisdom and piety. Archaeologist Clementina Panella, from Rome's Sapienza University, noted that the site lay between the Palatine and Velian hills, close to the Coliseum, the Arch of Titus and Via Sacra. Panella spoke of the artifacts and how they reflected a curious theological attitude of Numa Pompilius:

> Both wells were full of thousands of votive offerings and cult objects, including the bones of birds and animals and ceramic bowls and cups. There were no statues among the artifacts. That's because Numa forbade images of the gods in his temples, arguing that it was, impious to represent things Divine by what is perishable.[125]

The Fleets of Tarshish

I have already made brief mention of *Tarshish* and its ships. Due to the many references found in the Tanach, it is evident that the inhabitants of Tarshish are a sea-faring people.[126]

---

125 Richard Owen, "Unearthing Rome's King" (*Times On Line* UK/Oct 8th, 2007)

126 Psalms 48:7; Isaiah 2:16; 23:1; Ezekiel 27:25; Jonah 1:3

Biblically, their name is linked to maritime pursuits more than any other nation. Obviously, their fame lay in their skill as merchants sailing the coasts of the ancient Mediterranean. The design of their sailing vessels was so efficient that any craft fashioned in the same manner was referred to as a ship of Tarshish.

Fixing them geographically is not quite as simple since there are vastly differing opinions as to the exact location of *Tarshish.*

Josephus refers to Tharsus, though he is obviously speaking of Tarshish since he lists them among the sons of Javan. He also locates their homeland at a place the Greeks called *Cilicia*, which would later be the site of Tarsus, famous as the birthplace of the Apostle Paul. This area can be found on ancient maps as a strip of southern coastal land on what is now Turkey, just north of Cyprus.

Sefer HaYashar tells of Tarshish going to war just after Joseph becomes Viceroy in ancient Egypt. Chapter 50 relates that the children of Tarshish had waged a lengthy campaign against the children of Ishmael. The leaders of the Ishmaelites dispatch an appeal for military aide to Egypt. Pharaoh launches an assault against Tarshish with his new prime minister in command. Joseph is successful "and when the land of Tarshish was subdued, all the Tarshishites ran away, and came on the border of their brethren, the children of Javan".

What if the restless sea-going sons of Tarshish chose not to remain among their Greek kinsman? Perhaps the previously mentioned Tarsus, north of Cyprus, retained the name of these one-time inhabitants before they migrated westward. I will now crawl out on a limb of this genealogical tree and offer what I believe to be a better candidate for Tarshish – Spain.

> Tarshish was thy merchant by reason of the multitude of all kind of riches; with silver, iron, tin, and lead, they traded in thy fairs.
>
> – Ezekiel 27:12

A few Biblical commentaries make passing reference to Spain as Tarshish but usually dismiss it in favor of a site closer to the Greek Isles. I would like to suggest that, by virtue of their long history of seaworthiness, the Spanish are most likely the people of Tarshish. For instance, it is recorded in antiquity, a sea-going people arrived from Asia Minor on the Southwestern coasts of what is now Spain and founded a port called *Tartessus.*[127] Arguably, the name is very similar to Tarshish. Spain was famous for tin, gold and especially silver.[128] Even the prophet Jeremiah speaks of silver plates from Tarshish.[129] Spain's nautical heritage can be found in the name of the northernmost province called Navarra. It means boat. The name shares a linguistic root with the French *navire* and its related words such as navigate. An even more remarkable link to the sea-going origins of ancient *Hispania* can be found in the Hebrew word for boat – *spinah.*

Finally, we should consider the prophetical character of the many scriptural renderings that speak of the naval prowess of Tarshish and its dominance of the seas. Again, the same can be said for Spain. We remember our World History lessons regarding the mighty Spanish Armada who held sway over the seas until they were defeated by England in the summer of 1588. This victory of the English fleet for Queen Elizabeth radically shifted the global power base for years to

---

[127] *Merriam-Webster Geographical Dictionary* (Merriam-Webster Springfield, MA) p. 1161

[128] Will Durant, *The Life of Greece* (Simon & Schuster, NY, 1939) p. 169

[129] See Jeremiah 10:9

come.[130]

The Dodanim and the Fall of Troy

The Dodanim are only found twice in the Bible and both verses only mention their lineage from Javan, after the flood.[131] Herodotus speaks of a city in his day called *Dodona*. It was said to be the site of one of the most ancient oracles in Greece.[132] *The Aramaic text known as the Targum identifies Dodanim as Dardania,* a city on the Hellespont, also called the Dardanelles, the straits that separate the European continent from Asia. This same site is better known as the city of Troy.

The mythical founder of Troy was called Dardanus and the Trojans were sometimes called Dardanians.[133] There is even an Egyptian papyrus that describes a battle fought at Kadesh against the Hittites, relating that the *Dardenu* were their allies in battle.[134] Throughout his epic, *The Illiad,* the poet Homer calls the Trojans *Dardanians*. If the Dodanim of Genesis 10:4 and the Dardanians are one and the same then we have a Biblical connection to the people of Troy.

Not to muddy the historical waters, but the other name for ancient Troy was *Illium* (hence, *Illiad*). The name was derived from *Illis* who was the son of Tros. This *Illis* may

---

130 J.M. Roberts, *Penguin History of the World* (Penguin Books, London, UK, 1976) pp. 581-582

131 Genesis 10:4; I Chronicles 1:7

132 *Herodotus* 2:52, translated by David Grene (University of Chicago Press, Chicago, IL 1987) p. 154

133 Thomas Bulfinch, *The Golden Age of Myth & Legend* (Wordsworth Editions, UK, 1993) p. 254

134 *Life in Greece*, p. 35

have been named after *Elisha*, one of the sons of *Javan*, the Biblical ancestor of the Greeks.

Previously, I mentioned a king called Aeneas. He is the central figure found in a legendary poem called *The Aeneid*, Rome's national epic written around 30 BCE by Publius Vergilis Maro, known simply as Virgil. *The Aeneid* was very popular long after Virgil's death and seems to have taken on the force of history, even though the gods often intervene in the narrative.[135]

By the way, it is the words of Virgil in which we hear an eerie echo of Jacob's vision of Esau's angel ascending the heavenly ladder. He grew fearful when he learned that the domination of Esau would extend far into the future. In Virgil's poem, the god Jupiter pronounces:

> On [the Romans] I impose no limits of time or
>
> place. I have given them an empire that will know
>
> no end.

The historian Titus Livius appears to have drawn liberally from *The Aeneid* in his *Early History of Rome*. In Livy's account, Aeneas and his men set sail for a new home following the defeat of Troy. After some misfortunes, the weary Trojans eventually landed in Italy and forged an alliance with Latinus, a local chieftain. Latinus offered his daughter, Lavinia, in marriage to Aeneas who happily accepted. But the marriage caused a war. It seems that Latinus had already promised his daughter to Turnus, prince of Rutuli.

---

135 *The Aeneid of Virgil*, translated by Allen Mandelbaum (Bantam Books, NY, 1971)

In the war that ensued, both sides suffered heavy losses. Turnus is defeated and Latinus died in battle. Aeneas survived and married Lavinia. The couple is destined to be the ancestors of Romulus and Remus, the twins who will found the city of Rome.[136]

Another Amazing Parallel

Now, compare the legendary tale you've just read with a strikingly similar incident found in *Sefer HaYashar*. The book relates how the king named Angeas of Dinhabah is informed of a great beauty living in Kittim. He sent word that he wished to marry her. Since her father had passed away, the people of her city assented to the marriage. But another ruler in Italy, Turnus, had also heard of the woman's beauty and dispatched his messengers to ask for her hand. When Turnus is informed that he is too late, he decided the only one way to settle the matter and win the fair maiden was to wage war. Angeas dispatched his troops and was victorious. And he got the girl. The chapter closes by relating that Angeas and his people continually plundered Kittim.[137]

[136] *Livy: The Early History of Rome*, pp.3 5-36

[137] *Sefer HaYashar*, Chapter 60, pp.182-183

The parallels here are very intriguing. The text makes it clear that Angeas, made his capitol in, *"Dinhabah, which is Africa."* Consult a map and you'll see that Kittim (Italy) is closest to the northern Tunisia and Algeria on the northern coast of Africa. Modern Tunisia is where ancient Carthage was located. The Carthaginians waged constant war against the Romans. We know these campaigns as the Punic Wars that would one day bring a general named Hannibal to prominence.[138] But Carthage does not fit into our narrative; the city had not yet been built in the time of Angeas. A few miles west, along the same coastline, we find a place name which sounds like ancient *Dinhabah*. It is region called *Annaba*.

The Torah also references Dinhabah in Genesis 36:32:

> Bela son of Beor became king of Edom. His city was named Dinhabah.

---

[138] *The Penguin History of the World*, pp. 225-226

At the beginning of the thirty-sixth chapter of Genesis, the royal roll call takes a curious turn at verse thirty-one because the names of the rulers are not from the lineage of Esau. They are foreigners. According to the commentary known as *MeAm Lo'Ez*, the Edomites were unable to find anyone in their own ranks that they trusted or felt was capable to rule them and had to seek foreigners to install as their monarchs. Bela is among those kings who were not descendants of Esau. Many of the English translations imply that Bela's capitol was located somewhere in Edom. However, *Sefer HaYashar* also mentions this very same king and relates that he actually hailed from Dinhabah, a province ruled by Angeas and located on the North African coast:

> Therefore the sons of Esau swore, saying, From that day forward they would not choose a king from their brethren, but one from a strange land unto this day. And there was a man there from the people of Angeas king of Dinhabah; his name was Bela the son of Beor, who was a very valiant man, beautiful and comely and wise in all wisdom, and a man of sense and counsel; and there was none of the people of Angeas like unto him. And all the children of Esau took him and anointed him and they crowned him for a king....

> And the people of Angeas took their hire for their battle from the children of Esau, and they went and returned at that time to their master in Dinhabah.
>
> – Sefer HaYashar 57:40-44

Apparently, the Edomite clans had sought the services of Angeas and his army to serve as mercenaries. Edom's political connections with Angeas, his people and Bela is a vital link that connects Edom to the origins of Rome .

As stated earlier, I wanted to move all the geographical elements into place before introducing the key figure known as Zepho. It is here that we return to his saga recorded in *Sefer HaYasher*.

A Very Costly Funeral

We go back to the year 2255 on the Hebrew calendar (around 1505 BCE). The patriarch Jacob has just passed away at the age of 147. The 56th chapter of *Sefer HaYashar* records that as the sons of Jacob attempted to bury him in Hebron, Esau the brother of Jacob blocked the entrance to the sepulcher. A scuffle broke out and Esau was decapitated, his head rolling into the tomb. The scene escalated from a skirmish to an all-out battle. The children of Jacob defeated the children of Esau.

Among the captives is Zepho, the grandson of Esau. He is taken to Egypt in chains. Years later, when Joseph passes away, Zepho escapes from his Egyptian captors and flees along the western coast of Africa until he arrives in *Dinhabah*.

Angeas is still in power and appoints Zepho as "captain of his hosts." Angeas would come to regret this action. From the moment Zepho took command he lobbied daily to mount an all-out war against the Egyptians. He had an ulterior motive. Zepho really wanted revenge against the sons of Jacob who were still enjoying a peaceful existence among the Egyptians. Zepho continued to pound the drums of war against Egypt. The hatred for the Children of Israel had been learned at the knee of his father and grandfather – Eliphaz and Esau.

Angeas was afraid to take on the Egyptian armies knowing they also enlisted the Israelites as fighters. Zepho soon grew disenchanted with Angeas and turned against him and migrated to the coasts of Kittim. There he was hired by the locals to defend them against the likes of Angeas. It was during this time that Zepho not only proved himself on the battlefield but he became exceedingly rich.

It is at this point in our search for the Edom-Rome connection that we will see the pieces come together. In the 61st chapter of *Sefer HaYashar*, verses 24-25 states that Zepho, the grandson of Esau, became a leader of the people called the children of Kittim:

> And the children of Kittim saw the valor of Zepho...and they made Zepho king over them... they built him a very large palace for his royal habitation and made a large throne for him, and Zepho reigned over the whole land of Kittim and over the land of Italia fifty years.

The Jewish commentator, Abarbanel, makes this same connection as does *Yossipon*, a 10th century chronicle attributed to Joseph ben Gorion, which states that Zepho was crowned king of Kittim by its inhabitants.[139]

History and myth are easily mingled and assimilated with the passage of time. We have already seen a few examples where the two have become intertwined. If Zepho, grandson of Esau, became the first king to rule over all of Italy, it would come as no surprise that his subjects would want to know of his origins.

We can visualize Zepho, surrounded by his adoring minions as he recounted and traced his divine lineage, i.e., how G-d told Rebecca that noble leaders were in her womb. Zepho would have revealed that his regal ancestors were twins. All of those significant details could have evolved into a saga of twins born of a god and suckled by a she-wolf. I have speculated how the wolf wandered into this legend. It is not too much of a stretch to consider that the Hebrew word for wolf is *ze'ev*. Though not spelled the same, it sounds very much like Zepho.

Consider that this grandson of Esau would also include his grandfather's legacy of hatred for his brother Jacob. That attitude would be absorbed by the subjects of Zepho and grow into an instrument of terrible cruelty and oppression known as the Roman Empire.

The Beginning of Bondage

Zepho is also a key player in the pivotal decision by the Egyptians to enslave Israel. If you have ever wondered how Egypt could turn from being a nation grateful to Joseph for saving them from starvation, to becoming the evil overseers of slaves, *Sefer HaYashar* provides the answer.

Earlier, we learned that one of the reasons that Zepho

---

[139] See commentary on Daniel 2:40 in *Book of Daniel*, Artscroll Edition (Mesorah Publications, 1979) p. 106

turned against his former ally Angeas was the ruler's refusal to attack Egypt. After Zepho was securely ensconced as king over the children of Kittim, he mounted an invasion against Egypt and called upon his relatives, the Edomites to join him. He also enlisted the aid of the Ishmaelites in a massive onslaught that must have rivaled the Normandy Invasion. The Egyptians defended themselves by meeting Zepho and his army where they were camped, somewhere east of the Delta region.

The Egyptians feared that the Children of Israel would turn against them in battle. They reasoned that since the Israelites were blood relatives of Zepho and his Edomite band they would easily switch allegiance. The Egyptians decided to leave the Israelite contingent at the rear. However, when the onslaught of Zepho's combined forces proved too powerful, the Egyptians pulled back in retreat and called up the Israelites as reinforcements. Here's where the real trouble began.

The men of Israel enthusiastically joined the fray but the Egyptians kept running! The vastly outnumbered Israelites had to face the combined might of Kittim, Edom and the Ishmaelites without the Egyptian army. Israel called out to Hashem to strengthen them and He answered their prayer. The relatively small force of Israelites fought on with such fierceness that they repelled thousands of the enemy. The armies of Zepho began their own retreat. The Israelites turned the tide of battle in their favor and returned to Egypt. But not before tending to some unfinished business. When Israel encountered the still retreating Egyptian deserters they treated them as the enemy, executing them along the way. This act was to have enormous and far-reaching consequences.

The surviving Egyptian deserters returned to the king and recounted the terrible battle, conveniently omitting their own cowardly retreat. They lodged a formal protest against the Israelites. Hearing the report, Pharaoh believed that the Hebrews posed an internal threat to the nation. It was readily apparent to the king that, due to their prowess on the battlefield, the Hebrews would likely defeat his army in a civil war. They designed a plot to gradually destroy Israel.

Using the war with Zepho as a pretense, Pharaoh called on all citizens of Egypt to join in a national project to fortify the country against future assaults from foreign invaders. The crown proposed to improve the cities of Pithom and Rameses, in the Delta, to defend their eastern frontier. Pharaoh showed his support of the project by ceremonially laying the first brick. The plan worked and the nation rallied behind the king.

The children of Israel cheerfully worked alongside their Egyptian neighbors while Hebrew and Egyptian alike received their daily wages from the government-financed venture. Slowly, according to the plan, the Egyptian workers withdrew, forcing the Israelite laborers to take up the slack. Over a period of time, they found themselves alone on the construction and under the supervision of the Egyptians. That is how Israel became slaves in Egypt.[140]

We can now see how the Egyptians rationalized their enslavement of the Children of Israel.[141] The involvement of Zepho in the above episode is emblematic of his lineage. The attempt to blot out the Twelve Tribes is a pattern established by his grandfather, Esau.

In an earlier chapter, we saw how G-d had ordained this period of enslavement in Egypt. It is not my intent to

---

[140] *Sefer HaYashar* (Yosher /KTAV Publishing , Hoboken, NJ, 1993) pp. 169-171

[141] Even though G-d ordained the enslavement of Israel, Egypt would suffer greatly because their methods were harsher and far more cruel than necessary.

expound at length on a subject as sprawling as the Exodus. In my book, *Riddle of the Exodus*, I deal with the evidence that supports the veracity of the Biblical account and invite the reader to investigate the subject further.

However, I do wish to explore one aspect of the Exodus story that is completely misunderstood even by well meaning scholars – the actual length of the Egyptian exile. A less-informed reader might claim that the Torah contradicts itself by citing two separate passages regarding the actual years Israel spent in Egypt:

> Know for sure that your descendants will be foreigners in a land that is not theirs for 400 years. They will be enslaved and oppressed, but I will finally bring judgment against the nation who enslaves them, and they will then leave with great wealth.
>
> – Genesis 15:13-14

Now, compare it with:

> Now the sojourning of the children of Israel, who dwelt in Egypt, was four hundred and thirty years.
>
> – Exodus 12:40 (King James translation)

Which span of time is correct? Is it 400 years or 430 years?

The above verse from the Book of Exodus, as translated in the popular King James Version, is typical of nearly every English rendering. Yet those two figures are speaking of an all- encompassing period of time – from the time the promise was given to Abraham until the very day Israel marched out of Egypt. The actual number of years spent inside the borders of Egypt was *much less*. The Torah tells us that Jacob and his entire family migrated to Egypt and that his son Levi was already grown and had fathered Kohath. These two are, respectively, the great grandfather and grandfather of Moses. Exodus 6:16-20, gives us the total number of years these men lived, including the lifespan of Amram, the father of Moses. Factoring the age of Moses at the time of the Exodus and adding up the life-spans of his family reveals something quite startling:

Levi	137 years
Kohath	133 years
Amram	137
Moses	80 (at the time of the Exodus)
	487

Adding up their ages in consecutive fashion, as above, creates a problem. In reality the years of these men will overlap, especially in the case of Levi and Kohath, who were both alive when they entered Egypt. Also, none of these men would have fathered a son in the very last year of their life.

If we look at the lives of Abraham's son and grandson, Isaac and Jacob, we can see the words of Genesis 15:13 fulfilled. Isaac was always a foreigner, leading an almost nomadic life. Isaac was sixty when Jacob was born. In the case of Jacob, his years working under his shifty uncle, Laban, could definitely be characterized as servitude. When Jacob departed, he had become a man of great substance. Jacob also relocated several times, eventually settling in Egypt after his son Joseph became viceroy. Jacob was 130 years old when he arrived in Egypt.

G-d told Abraham that his *offspring* would be a stranger, so the counting of the 400 years *begins with the birth of his son, Isaac*:

From Isaac's birth until the birth of Jacob	60 years
From Jacob's birth until his arrival in Egypt	+130 years
	190 years

If we subtract 190 from 400, we get 210, the actual length of the exile in Egypt.

The number of years from the birth of Isaac until Jacob and family enters is 190 years:

Family enters Egypt	190 years
Length of exile	+210 years
	400 years

Seder HaOlam provides yet another calculation for the 210 years of the Egyptian exile:

Exile begins when Jacob migrates to Egypt	2238
Exodus occurs when Israel departs from Egypt	2448
Subtract the difference	210

The extra 30 years is reckoned by counting from *the very day that the promise was given to Abraham* – spoken 30 years before the birth of Isaac – hence, 430 years.

History also confirms this view of Abraham's descendants being under the sway of the Egyptian empire – even while living in Canaan. Egypt was at that time, a powerful force in the Levant. They often made incursions into the region inhabited by the first Hebrews. Recall how Abraham, during a time of famine, traveled to Egypt because that nation had withstood the effects of the event. Rabbi Aryeh Kaplan's *Living Torah*, reflects the reality that Abraham and his progeny were continually under the thumb of Egypt for as long as 430 years:

> The lifestyle the Israelites endured in Egypt had

thus lasted 430 years.

— Exodus 12:40

Chapter Fourteen

A CITY BECOMES AN EMPIRE

Zepho's influence gained a foothold in the Italian Peninsula, home of the coming Roman Empire. Kings would rule Edom before there was a king over Israel. Edom would also establish Zepho's worldview and his religion before the giving of the Torah. Just as Israel was entering a period of enslavement, which would shape them into a nation, Zepho would gain influence in a region that would allow his ideas – the ideas of Esau to be embedded with the world power.

Zepho would reign securely but, "...he walked in the ways of the children of Kittim and the wicked children of Esau, to serve other gods which his brethren, the children of Esau had taught him." [142]

Since Zepho was the grandson of Esau, there would have been an innate attraction to Baal worship. Early on, Esau had broken the heart of his mother Rebecca by marrying Canaanite women whose deity was Baal. Just a few miles from the shores of Italy, in ancient Carthage, there are ancient graveyards that yielded hundreds of urns containing the charred remains of children offered up in Baal worship.[143]

There are hints of other gods from the Middle East absorbed into the beliefs of the early Romans. Of course, Baal would become Apollo, while Adonis was the Greco-Roman name for Tammuz. Adonis is a corruption of the Semitic *adoni*, which means, "lord."

---

142 Ibid., 64:4

143 John Griffith Pedley, *New Light on Ancient Carthage* (University of Michigan Press, 1980)

Truth and Beauty

It is likely that the Kittim of the Italian Peninsula taught Zepho "enlightenment," a love of truth and beauty transmitted from their Greek ancestors. But it was still Greece's version of truth and beauty. The beauty of the Greeks was at odds with the Torah idea of beauty, something we can see in operation as far back as *Gan Eden*. Eve allowed her intellectual faculty to be distracted by the beauty of the tree. Torah, on the other hand, teaches that beauty comes from fulfilling the Divine plan. We understand this kind of beauty when we see a project completed or a when a complex plan comes together. It is no surprise that the idea of perfection in the Torah is linked to the idea of completion.

Zepho was drawn to thinking of those he encountered in his new home. He continued to practice the idolatrous ways of his grandfather's wives – women who worshipped Baal. But he also absorbed the beliefs of his new homeland. That amalgam of philosophies eventually spread throughout via the flourishing of what became Rome. Its influence would continue for centuries.

If this was enlightenment, why did it have the opposite effect on Israel? Rabbi Dr. Natan T. Lopes Cardozo offers this explanation:

> Midrashic literature often compares the Greek empire to "darkness which blinded the eyes of the Jews" (*Choshech ze Yavan*). The traditional interpretation is that the Jews in the days of the Maccabees were blinded by the Greek worship of the body and followed their example. It may, however, have a much deeper meaning. The Greeks are inventors of historical interpretation. Greek thinkers were among the first who tried to

> understand history in its more "scientific" form as reflected in the need to search for cause and effect. From the point of view of the Midrash, this approach blinded the Jews from reading history as a result of [Divine] emanations and their human response. It confused the deeper meaning of history, reversed effect with cause and darkened the clear insight of the Jews.[144]

Esau rejected the ethical lifestyle of his brother Jacob. Esau's reliance on self was taught to his grandson Zepho. Among the Kittim he would find a ready acceptance of that concept. The Torah later given at Mount Sinai would represent something totally alien to his subjects. They could not agree to complete submission (we call it faith in G-d) to the Lord of the Universe. Their reliance on logic sustained a strong drive for independence.

The concept of Democracy was rooted in that drive for individualism. On one hand these were a people who embraced hedonism to the extreme. On the other they believed happiness was secured through purely intellectual pursuits. The Greek intellectuals known as Sophists eventually "proved" that there were no gods. It was smart to do away with the whole pantheon — but the rot set in because, in this philosophy, there was no room for any kind of spiritual guidance. This sowed the seeds of their downfall. The late Rafael Eisenberg, in *Survival - Israel and Mankind*, sums it up thusly:

> The effect of the Sophist teaching was the final undermining of the authority of the gods, who were declared nonexistent. *And without gods there was no real basis for moral conduct.*

[144] Cardozo, "State of Israel-Thoughts to Ponder #69" (Root & Branch Association, Mar 11, 2001)

> Deprived of objective anchorage, moral principles were therefore all relative, as indeed the Sophists taught. For every ethical principle, its contrast was equally valid. Morality consists simply in satisfaction of desire.[145]

Eisenberg's book is a relevant and powerful work that documents the root causes of our global ills and how the very existence of our planet hinges on Israel's survival. And Israel's survival depends solely on their national belief in the words of the Torah. Eisenberg makes an impressive case against the weakness of all other philosophies and forms of government.

The Greek ideas should have brought a time of peace and tranquility. After all, a democracy meant everyone could pursue his or her own vision of happiness. But the opposite occurred. After defeating the Persians, the city-states of Athens and Sparta were locked in a power struggle for supremacy. They would prove easy prey for Alexander the Great. This Macedonian hero, schooled in Greek culture and philosophy, would conquer them and spread these ideas to the known world. After his death, the infighting continued among the Mediterranean city-states and they would fall victim to the emerging Roman Empire.

Though the Romans espoused the Greek concepts of truth, beauty and democracy, they were a brutal people. It should come as no surprise that the Jewish sages compared them to swine. As this unclean animal wallows in filth it shows a split hoof, which is the sign of a clean animal. But the pig can't meet the laws of *kashrut* since it does not also chew the cud. In the same way, the Roman Republic loved to proclaim noble virtues to the world; it was actually permeated with vast internal corruption and decadence.

---

145 *Survival: Israel & Mankind*, p.28

Israel, as it dispersed around the globe, positively influenced every nation and empire that has welcomed them during their wanderings. One example, cited in the works of the Roman historian Cicero, illustrates how the conquered Jews had a profound impact on their conquerors:

> "...the Jews brought to Rome in chains have succeeded in an amazingly short time in introducing and cultivating wisdom and ethics in all Roman cities."[146]

Cicero further relates how the Jews influenced the Romans so much that many began to see the futility of their endless and bloody domination. Apparently, that influence was temporary. Zepho established the tenets, learned from his grandfather Esau, among the inhabitants of the Italian Peninsula.

> The Romans had seen themselves as the successors of the Trojans and the Greeks – indeed, as the culminating empire for all time: empire without end.[147]

That doctrine flowed into Europe as the Roman Empire rose to power. Its effects on political and religious thinking can be charted from Constantine, continuing with the Byzantine Empire on to the Germanic Carolingians – then the Hapsburgs and eventually Nazi Germany, which proclaimed that it was the Holy Roman Empire reborn.

---

[146] Rabbi Petachya Menkin, *Pardes Petachya* (Tel Aviv, 1936)

[147] Cullen Murphy, *Are We Rome?* (Houghton Mifflin Company, New York, 2007) p.191

Chapter Fifteen

THE POLITICS OF ESAU

In Chapter Thirteen, we briefly referenced a commentary on Genesis 36:43 in the classical rabbinic texts known as Midrash Rabbah that prophetically linked Magdiel, one of the chiefs of Edom, to Emperor Diocletian, a ruler who radically changed the Roman Empire. The commentary relates how one of the Amoraim, Rabbi Ammi, had a dream on the day that Diocletian took power.[148] The rabbi told his contemporaries that Magdiel had become king and that there would be one more king over Edom.[149] If one more ruler followed Diocletian that would mean that his true successor, Constantine the Great was the "final" king over Edom. Though Rabbi Ammi saw these men as the last rulers of Rome, it may be that his prophetic insight actually revealed them as pivotal figures who heralded the end of one version of Rome and the birth of another, newer incarnation of the empire.

Diocletian made his mark on Roman history at a time of great transformation. The empire was in danger of collapsing. As emperor, he instituted massive reforms in the economy, the military and, most importantly, the way Romans were governed. By increasing the army and enlarging the civil service ranks, he elevated the bureaucracy and instituted Big Government. He was also known for wielding religious rhetoric in his quest for power. Though historians chart the end of the Roman Empire as

---

148 Rabbi Ammi is a name employed by some of the *Amoraim*. The latter is a designation given to a group of Talmudic scholars who lived between approximately 220 C.E. (the traditional date of the redaction of the Mishnah) and 370 in the Land of Israel and Babylonia.

149 Translated by Rabbi Dr. H. Freedman, *Midrash Rabbah - Genesis Volume II* (Socino Press, London & New York) p. 768

falling in the Fifth Century, it could be argued that it actually was reborn as something else that we now call Europe. Diocletian and Constantine were the midwives of that rebirth. They are credited by most contemporary historians for stabilizing the vastness that was Rome while forever changing the basic nature of the empire.[150]

Constantine was a benevolent dictator, if there is such a thing. He attempted to meld the Roman idea of conquest and autocratic rule with religion. This effort had been perfected centuries earlier by the founder of the empire – Zepho, the grandson of Esau. He was the first "benevolent dictator" of the Romim, on the River Tibreu.

Following the death of his father, Constantine took the reins of power. His influence was significant as author James Carroll reveals in his book *Constantine's Sword:*

> ...Constantine was the instrument of revolution in the religious imagination of the Mediterranean world, and eventually Europe. His political impact on Christianity is widely recognized, but his role as shaper of its central religious idea is insufficiently appreciated.[151]

Most of us are familiar with the famous story of Constantine

---

[150] *Western Civilization: The Continuing Experiment* (Houghton Mifflin Co., Boston & NY, 2005) p. 234

[151] James Carroll, *Constantine's Sword* (Houghton Mifflin, Boston, NY, 2001)
p. 173

and his victory at the Milvian Bridge, on the Tiber. The night before the battle, he had allegedly witnessed a cross in the sky hovering over a Latin phrase meaning, "In this Sign Conquer". Basking in bloody religious fervor that would make Esau proud, he eventually forced Christianity on the entire empire. Carroll likens the rule of Constantine as the 'second greatest story ever told' and reminds the reader that Constantine's adoption of Christianity led to a mass conversion in the "structures of culture, mind, politics, spirituality and even calendar."[152]

Constantine was like many of those world movers who came before and after him. In the beginning there was a tolerance toward other creeds as long as it suited his designs. But Constantine's tolerance for the Jews only went so far. As Carroll points out:

> Christianity went from being a private apolitical movement to being a shaper of world politics. The status of Judaism was similarly reversed.[153]

It was, after all, the influence of Constantine that kept alive the libel that the Jews killed Jesus. In his letter to the churches after the Council of Arelate, Constantine's warning about consulting the Jewish calendar exudes anti-Semitic bile:

> What right opinions can they have who, after the
>
> murder of the Lord, went out of their minds...[154]

---

[152] ibid. p. 171

[153] Ibid.

[154] Michael Grant, *The Jews in the Roman World* (Charles Scribner's Sons, New York, 1973) p. 284

The rule of Constantine would eventually bring about a repositioning of Jerusalem in the hearts and minds of the world. It was no longer regarded as a forgotten Roman province. It held a special place for the growing power of the Catholic Church. From that time on, the Papacy would continue to exert influence through the many permutations of the Roman Empire. There is no denying that Rome, as the Catholic Church, would extend its influence for hundreds of years and over much of the European continent.

It may not be coincidence that, centuries later, the new incarnation of Rome would emerge in the very same locale where Constantine began his ascent to power: the Roman province of Germania.

> From the time of Diocletian and Constantine until the formal disappearance of Roman Power in the West in 476, two rising institutions gradually took control of the western Mediterranean world. These new forces were, first, the Christian Church and, second, the German tribes who organized the kingdoms that inherited the western empire.[155]

Professor Carroll Quigley, who trained diplomats and world leaders at the Foreign Service School at Georgetown University, wrote that the rise of Hitler in Germany was possible because the Germans were still under the influence

---

[155] *A History of Civilization*, Vol I (Prentice Hall, Englewood Cliffs, NJ, 1967) p. 135

of Roman domination:

> The German continued to dream of that glimpse he had of that glorious, holy, eternal, imperial system before it sank. (The German) refused to accept that it was gone...All the subsequent failures of the German people from the failure of Otto the Great to Hitler in the 20th century have served to perpetuate and perhaps intensify the German thirst...for the totalitarian way of life.[156]

The imagery of Esau and Jacob grappling with one another vividly distills the historical struggle of opposing philosophies locked together. We have witnessed Greco-Roman concepts of government and religion reborn throughout the centuries – always emerging with Jacob's Torah principles clinging to them. Even a milestone such as the Magna Carta, drafted in 1215 AD was a mixture of the two philosophies. This historical document, which signaled a new beginning for the rights of the individual in England, was not welcome by the crown. King John immediately appealed to the Vatican to have it annulled. Of course, they were happy to oblige.

The French Revolution in 1789 was an event that actually paved the way for Napoleon's dictatorial thrust for conquest. This idea of Democracy would fuel the engine that powered the founding of our own country. But again its birth

---

[156] Carroll Quigley, *Tragedy & Hope* (MacMillan & Co. NY, 1966) pp. 409-411

represented the struggle between different ideologies.

Professor Quigley agreed with those who believed it was their duty to preserve the Western way of life at any cost. He had intimate knowledge of the various Round Table Groups in America and England. One of them, formed in 1919, was the Royal Institute of International Affairs.

Cecil Rhodes, the fabulously wealthy diamond magnate, aided and abetted the creation of this organization with like-minded individuals to preserve and expand the British Empire as well as their own ideas of what was right and good for mankind. Rhodes was an ardent student of John Ruskin who espoused a belief system that found its roots in ancient Greece.

Prior to World War II, the Council on Foreign Relations, the Institutes of Pacific Relations and a group called Union Now were formed by the powerful men who esteemed these ideologies. The latter, based in England, was instrumental in conceiving the so-called "three bloc world." They envisioned a new Europe with England on one end of the continent and the Soviet Union at a safe distance on the other. An Adolf Hitler-ruled bloc of countries would provide a necessary protective buffer in between. Neville Chamberlain was at their beck and call, shuttling across the continent seeking to appease Adolf Hitler.

Union Now was also under the misguided impression that Hitler was only interested in his immediate neighborhood. He was like the farmer who said that he only wanted the property that bordered his own land. If Poland and Czechoslovakia refused to give in, they were standing in the way of peace. Chamberlain finally extracted a promise from the Czech government to grant "autonomy" to Germans living in the Sudetenland.

Tragically, Chamberlain returned to England proclaiming, "Peace in our time." Hitler's tanks rolled into Czechoslovakia shortly afterwards.

It was this kind of treachery that eventually led to World War II and the Holocaust.[157] The European powers and anti-Torah Liberals are using this very same model today. They are telling Israel to dole out whole portions of its land under the guise of granting "autonomy" to the Palestinians. By not doing so, Israel is accused of standing in the way of peace and democracy.

---

[157] *Tragedy & Hope*, pp. 580-583

Chapter Sixteen

THE MESSIAH OF ESAU

The natural physical resemblance of Jacob and Esau was a prophetic model that revealed how the world would be shaped by these two nobles from the womb of Rebecca.

Jacob, as the Jewish nation, has struggled to survive the dominance of Esau, in the form of Western civilization. The Jews have for centuries faithfully anticipated the arrival of the Messiah. Esau came first, ruled first and offered up his own messiah – one who is a poor reflection of the true messiah. The messiah of Esau is an image that gained a foothold in history, surviving even to this day.

Jesus is the messiah of Esau, but why is he so appealing to the Western mind and Christianity?

It may be that this messiah embodies the defining traits of Esau. Primarily, Jesus represented a deity that was tangible, unlike the invisible G-d of the Jews. That appeals to the materialism of Esau. Then there is the need for instant gratification so evident in the manner in which Esau gulped down his bowl of red – Jesus was a messiah one didn't have to wait for – he had already come.

Passion vs. Reason

Mel Gibson's controversial film *The Passion* stirred millions of Christians with its graphic imagery of a beaten and bloody Jesus. Audience members told of being moved to tears, expressing how they had never grasped the extent of his suffering. Others spoke of an emotional response so strong that their faith was renewed.

None of this is surprising since this is one of the hallmarks of

Christianity in that it stirs the emotion but is divorced from the intellect. It is the cognitive dissonance of Esau that tunes out anything that fails to match his feelings. *His heart is the standard by which he measures all things.* Western literature and song are rife with the mantra of "follow your heart." It is the core message of thousands of popular films. The protagonist, faced with an existential fork in the road is advised by a mentor to "follow your heart." This is what often separates the Christian from the Jew.

It might seem that this would make the Jew cold and distant while the Christian is all hugs and brotherly embraces. I would submit that anyone who holds this view has never enjoyed the warmth of a Shabbat table or counted the number of Jewish charities that exist. Obviously, there is an abundance of worthy Christian outreach to the poor and needy. But history runs red with blood-soaked Christian emotionalism. There has never been a Jewish Inquisition or Crusade. It is this emotional component that fuels such strong conviction in the idea of a Suffering Messiah. His required demise on the cross is so pivotal to Christianity that without it, there would be no Christianity.

True Judaism urges one to employ reason, while Christianity is based on emotionalism. Preachers, ignorant of Torah teachings, often rant about the so-called legalism of the rabbis. To further their lopsided worldview, the same preachers would have us check our brains at the door of their churches. On the other hand, the Torah model for living is faith that employs a healthy balance of fervor with logic---not one to the exclusion of the other:

> Religions or spiritual systems which attempt to
>
> connect to Oneness solely through spiritual means,

> while disdaining the particulars of the created world, insult God's detailed creation, the awesome cosmos. In contrasts, the Torah system teaches us how to mediate between the details of created world and the Oneness of God, thereby showing ultimate respect for both poles of reality.[158]

Within the first pages of Genesis, this concept is repeated throughout the creation account. After each period of vast and epic formation, G-d plainly calls His handiwork good.

Cross Heirs

At this point, it would be instructive to revisit the Offering of Isaac. The *Akeidah* is an essential aspect of Jewish belief but it was corrupted by Christian theologians and became a core of their doctrine to support the crucifixion.

Typically Christians are taught that this unique event is a "foreshadowing" of Jesus. For example the popular Scofield Bible and its commentaries are ripe with metaphor as they quote and connect various New Testament themes. Isaac is labeled a type of savior, "obedient to death." Abraham is the Father who "spared not his own son but delivered him up for us all."

---

158 Batya Gallant, *Stages of Spiritual Growth* (Devora Publishing, Jerusalem/NY, 2010) p. 140

However, in an unusual casting choice, Jesus is allowed double symbolic duty. He is both personified as Isaac – and also the ram caught in the thicket. The problem with this imaginative symbolism is that theologians try to have it both ways.

Is Jesus symbolic of Isaac, or is he the ram?

If one describes experiences in the metaphoric realm, there should be some consistency. Isaac and Jesus are portrayed as being obedient to death, but then Jesus transforms from Isaac into the ram in the thicket and *dies in his own place*. Those who proffer this confusing allegory never explain the leap from one symbol to the other. I could play this same game and arbitrarily pronounce that the ram in the thicket is symbolic of replacement theology.

Any rabbi worth his *semicha* will tell you that for thousands of years this incident, known as the *Akeidah*, was the last and the greatest of ten trials that Abraham would experience. It teaches a number of profound lessons, the first of which is the utter faithfulness of Abraham. Most profoundly it teaches that the Creator *rejects death as a form of worship*.

In the context of the time and place, Abraham was not some oddball loner who secretly attempted to barbeque his son – in fact, everyone would eventually hear of it. The Oral Tradition reveals a interesting detail about the death of Sarah. She was so overcome with joyful relief when informed that Isaac had not died on Moriah that she suffered a heart attack and died! That's why the account of Sarah's burial, in the Torah, is placed immediately after the story of Isaac's offering.

There is yet another lesson that the Jewish sages teach regarding this unusual episode and it is found in the original Hebrew of Genesis 22: 14:

Vayikra Avraham shem-hamakom hahu Adonay Yir'eh asher ye'amer hayom behar Adonay yera'eh.

This translates as "Abraham named the place 'G-d will See'." Today, it is therefore said, "On G-d's Mountain, He will be seen."

What did G-d see?

Chazal (Jewish Sages) teach that the *MizbeaH* (stone altar) where Isaac was bound is the very same place that Adam was created. It is also the site where Cain and Abel brought their offerings and, after the Flood, Noah would journey to the same mountain to bring an offering.

The site would later serve as pillow for Jacob, the son of Isaac. He would dream of a heavenly ladder and announce that, "*surely G-d is in this place.*" Solomon built *Beit HaMikdash* (The First Temple) on this mount and Jacob's pillow was the *Kedosh Ha Kedoshim* or Holy of Holies on which was placed the Ark of the Covenant.

In Abraham's day, the city of *Shalem* was near this altar. The ruler of *Shalem* was Melchizedek who was actually Shem, the son of Noah. After the *Akeidah*, G-d would honor the absolute faithfulness of Abraham and He would forever *YiReh* (see) the ashes of the sacrificed ram substituted for Isaac. Of course, we know the entire area surrounding this sacred site as *YiRehSHaLem*.

Through their own willful ignorance, countless theologians have allowed the smoke from the *Akeidah* to cloud their vision. They have failed to grasp the profound truth on the page of the holy text. G-d sanctioned properly executed sacrifices so that the animal would serve as a substitute for the one giving the offering. In the *Akeidah*, the Creator underscores the fact that this offering is a partnership between G-d and the Jewish people.

In the future, when Israel would finally settle the land and build the Temple, a Jew would bring an *olah* (elevated burnt offering) and he was to identify with it. The Creator looks upon our actions in tandem with the intent of our heart. He does not see the ashes of an animal – G-d only sees the symbolic remains of Isaac.

This is the model for the true living sacrifice: to offer one's very existence in a life that continues in faithful service to G-d and to humanity.

Christians are taught that Jesus is their example. But instead of living a full life of teaching, caring and re-shaping the world, his lot was to be slaughtered in the prime of his life with chaos falling upon his fellow Jews. The symbolism that surrounded the *Akeidah* was never meant to be the template for a bloody, human sacrifice. On the contrary, it provided the daily mechanism that reinforced the concept that the Jewish people were personally responsible for their service to G-d. It is not Jesus' faith that saves the world, it is the faith of the Jew who believes G-d and offers his everyday existence to repair and reshape the world. True salvation saves the physical world that the Creator declared was good and the process shapes the soul.

The Christian commentary diminishes Abraham's act of supreme faithfulness and turns him into some doddering fool, incapable of doing things properly. It negates the concept of *G-d will see* as expressed in Genesis 22:14. Replacement Theology suggests that our Creator shuffled the deck and changed the rules. Indeed, theologians would have us believe that all of those animals, for hundreds of years, were being slaughtered to simply reinforce the idea of an eventual final slaughter necessary to save mankind.

It begs two questions.

1) Where is the concept Messiah who dies for mankind found in the Torah, Prophets or Writings?

Everything that Israel is to understand and to know about the Messiah is presented with clarity. He is a human king and a great leader who will restore Israel under Torah – not die horribly on a pole.

2) How far are theologians willing to take this metaphorical template of Jesus as the spotless sacrifice?

The Replacement-colored commentaries constantly bombard the reader on this matter. Of course, one could respond that this was a reference to Jesus' supposedly divine soul and sinless nature. If the entire sacrificial system has been a shadow and type, a forerunner of the sacrifice of Jesus – and if he allowed himself to be led to slaughter like all those animals before him – then why was he not slaughtered according to strict guidelines as commanded by G-d?

The blemish-free state of these animals was more than just cosmetic; the physical wholeness of the animal was vital to the sacrifice being *kosher*. To insure that the offering was indeed, perfect, the animal had to be killed in the proper manner. By pinching on a specific artery of the neck, the creature passed out, then came the expert cut of the *shochet's* blade. The animal felt no pain. Compare this to what is recorded in the gospels regarding the crucifixion and death of Jesus.

If you were one of those who saw the vivid cinematic recreation in Mel Gibson's *The Passion*, surely there is no doubt that Jesus' death at the hands of the Romans was anything but painless. By all accounts, he was flayed and beaten into bloody pulp before he ever got to the cross. Finally, he was nailed to a wooden beam, raised up and left to slowly suffocate in the heat of the day.

This leads to another question.

If Isaac was a shadow and type of Jesus' passion, where is the savagery and torture that Isaac should have experienced? None of his blood was shed. Isaac even asked his father to bind him securely so that he wouldn't move and spoil the sacrifice.

How can the misery and brutality of the crucifixion be the perfect, spotless sacrifice?

This emphasis on death and the grave is what distinguishes Judaism from Christianity. The constant refrain from the pulpit is the "Death, Burial and Resurrection of Christ."

Judaism is all about *Life* and *Tikun HaOlam*, the repair of the world. It is part of the Divine plan realized in the oft-repeated phrase that the Torah is an Owner's Manual for mankind. It was given to the Jewish People so that they could teach the world *how to live* full and vital lives – not how to die.

When Israel fell short of their mission as a Kingdom of *Kohanim* (priesthood), the Church would have us believe that G-d broke His Covenant and abandoned what He called "a treasured people." (Deut 26:18). Replacement Theology takes an even harsher view by propagating the sad image of the Jewish People punished because they "killed Jesus."

None of these ideas are supported in the Torah, Prophets or the Holy Writings. Think about it. Israel suffered violently while under Egyptian bondage. They were attacked by the Assyrians. Later, their Holy Temple was burnt to the ground; they were slaughtered and led, in chains, to Babylon. But those tragedies occurred before Jesus ever appeared on the scene.

This damnable heresy of Israel being punished for the death of the Christian messiah only takes on the illusion of reality if one *selectively* reads the curses and warnings to Israel from G-d and His prophets. By selective, I mean that one simply scans any of the curses then ceases to read any further.

I challenge the reader to go to any of the prophetical warnings for Israel and test this. For instance, read Deuteronomy 28:15. As you inspect the exhaustive list of calamities pronounced by Moses you will note the warnings offer an eerie vision of the Holocaust – but don't stop there! Read on to Chapter 30 and take note that after the blessings and the curses, Moses offers an amazing panorama of G-d's forgiveness and thrilling promise to His people:

> There shall come a time when you shall experience all the words of blessing and curse that I have presented to you. There, among the nations where God will have banished you, you will reflect on the situation. You will then return to God your Lord, and you will obey Him, doing everything that I am commanding you today. You and your children [will repent] with all your heart and with all your soul. God will then bring back your remnants and have mercy on you. God your Lord will once again

> gather you from among all the nations where He scattered you. Even if your diaspora is at the ends of the heavens, God your Lord will gather you up from there and He will take you back. God your Lord will then bring you to the land that your ancestors occupied, and you too will occupy it. God will be good to you and make you flourish even more than your ancestors."
>
> — Deuteronomy 30:1- 6

This theme is repeated throughout the Torah, Prophets and Holy Writings. The warnings and curses are like a preamble to the loving, forgiving and wholly redemptive promises of G-d towards Israel. Certainly, the Jewish people were punished for not keeping their agreement at Sinai to "do and hear" all that the Torah commanded.

There is nothing, not even in the weakest English translation of the s0-called Old Testament, to support the concept that G-d changed His mind or forever turned His back on the Jewish people.

To entertain such thinking is to accuse the Master of the Universe of being a failure, forced to revise some flawed cosmic scheme.

Chapter Seventeen

THE HANDS OF ESAU AND THE VOICE OF JACOB

As shocking as it may sound, pure Democracy, in its undiluted form, does not quite work in the Creator's plan for Israel. This is not to suggest that Democracy is evil. In fact, the Torah is replete with what we might term democratic principles. Even though there is great importance placed on the priesthood, their authority was confined to the daily operation and support of matters pertaining to the Temple. There was even a kind of checks and balances as represented in the king, the prophet and Sanhedrin. It was the 71 elders known as the Sanhedrin, established at Sinai, which functioned as a combination Congress and Supreme Court. The Sanhedrin interpreted Torah law, rendered judgments in high-level cases and matters of national interest. The courts as represented in this system were innovative in the ancient world and remain our model for justice today. Anyone charged in a crime could not be tried unless they had counsel.

Because the Torah Law was supreme, even the king was subject to the Sanhedrin. A monarch would have to stand trial in a case brought against him by a private citizen. Laws enacted by the Sanhedrin had to be accepted by the majority of the Tribes. Entrance to the august body was open to anyone, although their credentials had to reflect a vast knowledge of Torah, astronomy, mathematics, anatomy and medicine. Additionally, they had to possess great sagacity, solid character, compassion and humility.

The only reason that our own nation has lasted this long is because our Founding Fathers had the wisdom to incorporate actual Torah precepts into the schematics of our government – especially the belief that laws are derived from the Creator. A major flaw inherent in pure Democracy, devoid of belief in G-d, is relativism. Translated into matter-of-fact language, it means the mob rules. Democracy insists on consent while Torah insists on wisdom. The modern state of Israel will become a model nation when it eventually implements G-d's blueprint for government found in the Torah.

The twins are still wrestling with one another, but now the dust from this struggle is choking modern Israel. It has given rise to such a peculiar mental state that author Paul Eidelberg coined the word "Demophrenia" to explain it. I cannot articulate this ironic dilemma any better than Mr. Eidelberg, a former professor of Political Science at Bar-Ilan University in Israel:

> By emulating a democracy that pays lip service to Christianity, Israel's government has unwittingly conditioned Gentiles to expect the Jews to abide by the most unassertive and self-effacing Christian precepts: turn the other cheek, love your enemies, do not resist evil. And to the extent that [Israel] has adhered to these benign and apolitical Christian precepts – *unpracticed by any Gentile nation* – it not only has forsaken Judaism, it has also repressed the sense of outrage among Jews whose loved ones have been the victims of Arab terrorists.[159]

The hypocrisy of our Western press and leadership is blatantly exhibited whenever Israel attempts to defend itself against the constant threat of terrorism within their own borders.

---

[159] Paul Eidelberg, *Demophrenia: Israel & the Malaise of Democracy* (Prescott Press, Lafayette, LA, 1994) p. 164

Though the government of Israel likes to boast that it is one of the few democracies in the Middle East, there is a craziness that infects the process in the name of democracy. This is demonstrated by the fact that an Arab member of the Knesset can decide on the issue of "Who is a Jew?" If, somehow, the Arabs became a majority in the Israeli parliament, they could actually vote in an Arab government! I have to quote Eidelberg again when he says that the present situation:

> ...confirms the proposition that politics and democracy in Israel are in the most advanced state of decay. This decay is providential; for one of the world-historical functions of democracy is to destroy all man-made ideologies and then self-destruct.[160]

Professor Eidelberg is not a prophet of doom. He is quick to point out that there is a growing body of scientists, mathematicians and economists in Israel who are espousing the Torah as the prototype of genuine knowledge. Observant Jewish thinkers have applied Torah basics to such subjects as Quantum mechanics, Chemistry and Biology with startling results. While these brilliant scholars are tapping into the profound truths of the Torah, their secular brothers are achieving remarkable success in the material realm.

---

160 ibid p.164

Chapter Eighteen

MESSIAH NATION

In late 2009, Dan Senor and Saul Singer created a stir with the publication of *Start-Up Nation*, their eye-opening account of Israel's amazing success in the economic and technological realm. How, the authors asked, could such a small country, constantly under the threat of war, manage to produce more successful start-up companies than larger, so-called stable countries like Japan, China and the United Kingdom? They go on to cite unexpected statistics to make their case:

- There are more Israeli companies listed on the NASDAQ than all the companies in Europe.
- In the year 2008, per capita venture capital investments in Israel were 2.5 times greater than the U.S., more than 30 times greater than Europe and 80 times than China and 350 than in India.
- Israel's economy has grown faster than the average for a developed country in the world since 1995.

Google's CEO and chairman, Eric Schmidt, Microsoft's Steve Ballmer, financial whiz Warren Buffett and others trumpeted the marvelous benefits of investing in Israel in the book. For decades, Buffett resisted buying a foreign company but he broke his own rule and spent over 4 billion dollars to acquire an Israeli business – at the onset of the 2006 Lebanon War.[161]

Start-Up Nation is an inspiring read. The book celebrates the innovation and boldness of Israel's tech and entrepreneurial

---

[161] Dan Senor and Saul Singer, *Start-Up Nation* (Twelve Books, NY, 2009) pp. 11-15

sector. Just one example of the revolutionary ventures coming out of Israel is the "Pill-cam" invented by Gavriel Iddan, founder of Given Imaging. He developed a camera for medical application that is the size of a pill. When swallowed by the patient, it transmits as many as eighteen black and white images a second from the intestinal tract.

Authors Senor and Singer attempt to nail down what makes the Israeli business model so unique. They discovered that the one pervasive factor shared by these entrepreneurs was their combat experience in the Israeli Defense Forces. Many of them, still in their early twenties, were given vital command positions in the field. In the heat of combat, they were forced to be resourceful and creative. Their initiative often caused them to question authority to achieve objectives – saving lives. These valuable administrative skills and the camaraderie they experienced proved applicable in the business world.

> Indeed, what makes the current Israeli blend so powerful is that it is a mashup of the founders' patriotism, drive and constant consciousness of scarcity and adversity and the curiosity and restlessness that have deep roots in Israeli and Jewish history.[162]

In the closing pages of Senor and Singer's book, we read of the founders of modern Israel and how their idealism and brashness, in the face of impossible odds, resulted in a nation and culture that was, in every sense of the word – "start-up."

As much as I enjoyed their book, I found it lacked one key component that is essential to the success story of modern Israel: *G-d is missing from the book.*

---

[162] Ibid., page 228

Sadly, the rare mention of anything remotely religious in *Start-Up Nation* is a set of statistics used to shore up the mistaken notion that the *haredi* populace could hinder the growth of the Israeli economy – thus giving the book a decidedly anti-religious bias. The authors also describe the *haredim* as "Ultra-Orthodox." This is a hazy designation at best, one that means different things to different people. To the casual first-time visitor to Israel, any Israeli sporting side-locks and a *kippah* is Ultra-Orthodox. I prefer the term Torah-observant Jew.

The idea that Torah-observant Jews are in the way of progress is simply not the reality in modern Israel. One example is my friend, Gedaliah Gurfein, an observant Jew who is a successful entrepreneur specializing in web-based and computer-related start-ups. His efforts got him written up in *Forbes* magazine[163]. His company is located in *Har Hotzvim*, a business hub in Jerusalem where one can find the offices for companies like Intel and other high-tech businesses. I asked Gedaliah how other companies like his regarded the Observant Jew:

> The tech companies employ everyone from knitted-kippah types, like me, to the young guys from Mea Shearim, wearing a frock coat. I know that we are not regarded as being in the way of progress. These guys all demonstrate a wonderful sophistication for the work and an easy grasp of technology. The secular bosses in these companies appreciate the attitude of a religious guy who believes that wasting time on the job is no different than stealing from their employer."

163 "The Accidental Deal", Joanne Gordon, Nov 15, 1999, also see InfoWorld "Mobile Technology Takes Dispensers On-Line" by Ephraim Schwartz, August 28th, 2000, p.29

In many respects, the young secular Israeli who serves in the IDF and goes on to conquer the business world is approaching the Torah mandate. Their high-tech solutions to the problems in science and medicine are truly shedding light into a darkened world. The authors of *Start-Up Nation*, who extol the virtues of the bold new entrepreneurs, seem to think that these young men and woman are at odds with religious ideas. I would submit that their innovation, bravery and *sekel* (wit) is proof that these young veterans do recognize they are from a nation of prophets and holy warriors. As long ago as 1993, a study conducted by the prestigious Guttman Institute of Applied Social Research, revealed that the long-held belief that Israeli society was sharply divided between the secular and Torah-observant is no longer the reality. One of the more startling findings revealed that nearly two thirds of all Israelis believe that there is a God, while 55 percent believe in the literal revelation of the Torah by God at Sinai.[164]

In 2011, I attended a nano-technology conference in Tel-Aviv. I saw innovative applications of this science being demonstrated by young Israelis who were completely comfortable talking about G-d, Torah and Israel. Apparently, the old disconnect between the young Israeli entrepreneurs and their Torah-observant brother is dissolving away. In the description of Jacob and Esau, in the womb of their mother, we find an amazing hint of the character of the future leadership of Israel, the one called Messiah. The verse tells us they were twins but the Hebrew phrase carries another meaning. It can also be read "they were perfect."

Both brothers excelled in wisdom and strength. The elder Esau used his talents to found a warring dynasty while Jacob

[164] Daniel J. Elazar, (1996) "How Religious Are Israeli Jews?" Jerusalem Center for Public Affairs, Retrieved June 19, 2011: http://www.jcpa.org/dje/articles2/howrelisr.htm

became the patriarch of a Holy Nation.

We already know that the template for that dynamic was set even further back in time, with Cain and Abel. The time is ripe to reconcile that historic rift as thousands of Torah-believing Jews return to their land and enlarge on the mandate from Sinai to be a *light to the nations*.

The near future holds great promise. Modern Jews in Israel are turning into faithful brothers, patiently waiting for those who will return to Torah values. Their secular brother will, like Joseph's brothers, soon recognize a loving and regal brother crowned with G-d's wisdom standing before them and they will see a mirror image of themselves.

The wrestling of Jacob and Esau will soon become an embrace as they realize that they are the sum of all those who came before them – those who have struggled with G-d and man to overcome their own self-centered nature. The brotherly embrace will meld the two into one cohesive figure. In their monumental journey through history, they will have ultimately unlocked the eternal truths of Torah that will enable Israel to lead all of humanity into an exciting new world. The Jewish People will rectify the mistakes of the past and become the true Israel.

Not a Start-Up Nation – but a Messiah Nation.

CONCLUSION

The Torah Sages teach that every nation has an angel. When the Creator decrees that a nation will fall, that angel is put to flight. There is one vital difference between Edom and Israel. According to the Torah Sages, Israel has no angel. It is directly under the influence of the Creator. On the other hand, Edom has rejected any such direction, opting for autonomy that is free of the Creator. The result, as history vividly teaches, is constant warfare, the decline in morality and the fall of empires.

It may take another devastating war or some horrendous display of technology gone awry, but mankind will eventually recognize the folly of denying the direction of the Creator.

Adam discovered this, long ago in *Gan Eden*. Because he chose to descend into the physical realm, Adam set the parameters for the existence of mankind from that point on. He created a situation where achieving both the spiritual and physical would come through the "sweat of our brow."

Why the brow?

The real struggle always begins in our brow – our thinking. It is there that we must destroy idols – anything that we elevate above G-d.

Throughout history, those who have moved mankind forward have accepted this sweat of the brow – this intellectual struggle. The greatest tool in this struggle is Torah. It was always embedded in the divine blueprint to spread the Creator's precepts for a better world to the far corners of the earth. The scattering of the Jewish people among the nations has effectively revealed the light of Torah worldwide. It is up to humanity to realize that we all reap the benefits of its wisdom. When that happens, there will be a renewed level of understanding and knowledge coupled with a purer form of worship, free of idols. Physics, medicine, and all the sciences will take a quantum leap and we will attain a level unrealized in the past. Our awareness of our place in the universe and our partnership in creation will finally reflect a higher, more rational state. For all will come to see that it is a most rational thing to believe in the G-d of Israel.

If we look at Exodus 4:21, there is a statement that has always struck me as astonishing. G-d instructs Moses to inform the pharaoh that "Israel is my son, my first-born." Since the Jewish People are G-d's first-born, it must then follow that all other nations are the younger siblings.

In the beginning, the older brother Cain failed to be concerned for the welfare of Abel and the result was a world plunged into chaos. In Cain we saw how the elder squandered his gifts and failed the ultimate test when he rejected responsibility for his brother.

The Creator has never ceased to inquire about the younger brother. *He continues to ask the first-born.* We can, literally, thank G-d that Jacob responded to that eternal question. He redeemed the position of the First-Born when he took on the role of Israel.

We can rest in the Creator's faith in the Jewish People demonstrated by his bestowal of the Torah upon them – the ultimate user's guide for humanity. The question to the elder brother carries a supreme and simple cure for the ills of the planet. His faith in this Holy Nation guarantees that they will ultimately fulfill their destiny as their brother's keeper.

> And in the days of these kings shall the God of heaven set up a kingdom, which shall never be destroyed: and the kingdom shall not be left to

other people, but it shall break in pieces and consume all these kingdoms, and it shall stand for ever.

— Daniel 2:43

ACKNOWLEDGMENTS

I thank the Creator, the G-d of Abraham, Isaac and Jacob for allowing me to bring you this book. It is my hope that some wisdom has graced its pages. It is the result of a journey that began for me when I met the late Vendyl Jones, of blessed memory, in the late '90s. I was exposed to his love of G-d, his enthusiasm for Torah, the genuine affection he had for the Jewish People as well as his unstinting support for the State of Israel. More than ever, I appreciate his patience and good cheer. The manuscript for *Blood Brother* has been read and commented on by a number of friends and scholars but the three that I want to especially mention are Rabbi Chaim Richman, International Director the Temple Institute in Jerusalem, Rabbi Michael Shelomo Bar-Ron founder of the *Ohel Moshe* Society. Others who encouraged and aided this endeavor include fellow Noahide Andy Overall, Professor Paul Eidelberg, Jerry Robins and Aryeh Wells. Their salient comments were a most helpful. Authors Isaac Mozeson and Eugene Narrett were also of great help. Thanks to Renee Crowell, a long-time friend and our Lightcatcher Books representative in Israel. Finally, the completion of the book would literally not have been possible without my wife, Carol. In addition to designing the cover and the layout, it was she who urged me to expand the article, *The Angel of Edom* into the book you now hold in your hands. To all of you, *Todah Rabbah*.

BIBLIOGRAPHY

Aeneid of Virgil. Translated by Allen Mandelbaum. New York: Bantam Books, 1971

Antiquities of the Jews, The Life and Works of Flavius Josephus. Translated by William Whiston. Philadelphia: The John C. Winston Co., 1980

Arnott, Peter D. *The Romans and Their World*. New York: St. Martins Press, 1970

Artscroll Tanakh. Brooklyn, New York: Mesorah Publications, 1988

Authentic Annals of the Early Hebrews, aka the *Book of Jasher*, aka *Sefer HaYashar.* Compiled by Wayne Simpson. Springdale, AR: Lightcatcher Books, 2003

Bar-Ron, Rabbi Michael Shelomo. *Guide For the Noahide*. Springdale, AR: Lightcatcher Books, 2011

Bulfinch, Thomas. *The Golden Age of Myth & Legend*. Hertfordshire, UK: Wordsworth Editions, 1993

Book of Daniel, The Artscroll Tanach. Brooklyn, NY: Mesorah Publications ,1988

Cardozo, Nathan Lopes "State of Israel-Thoughts to Ponder #69" Root & Branch Association, Mar 11, 2001

Carroll, James *Constantine's Sword*. Boston/NY: Houghton Mifflin, 2001

Chumash, Hirsch Edition. Trans. by Daniel Haberman. Jerusalem, New York: Feldheim/Judaica Press, 2002

Harper, Robert Francis. *The Code of Hammurabi, King of Babylon.* Chicago, Il: University of Chicago Press, 1904

Complete Works of Flavius Josephus. Grand Rapids, MI: Kregel Publications, 1960

Culi, Rabbi Yaakov *The Torah Anthology* (*MeAm Lo'ez*) Books One and Two. Trans. by Rabbi Aryeh Kaplan. NY/Jerusalem: Moznaim Publishing, 1989

De Selincourt, Aubrey. *Livy: The Early History of Rome*. New York: Penguin Classics, 1981

Durant, Will. *The Life of Greece*. New York: Simon & Schuster, 1939

Eidelberg, Paul. *Demophrenia: Israel &the Malaise of Democracy.* Lafayette, LA: Prescott Press, 1994

Eidelberg, Paul. *Toward a Renaissance of Israel and America*. Springdale, AR: Lightcatcher Books, Springdale, AR, 2009

Eisenberg, Rafael. *Survival: Israel & Mankind.* Ed. by Abraham Sutton. Jerusalem/NY: Feldheim, 1991

Fohrman, Rabbi David. *The Beast That Crouches at the Door*. Jerusalem / New York: Devora Publishing, 2007

Gallant, Batya. *Stages of Spiritual Growth*. Jerusalem/New York: Devora Publishing, 2010

Gardiner, Alan. *Egypt of the Pharaohs*. New York: Oxford University Press, 1961

Grant, Michael. *The Founders of the Western World*. New York: Scribner, 1991

Grant, Michael. *The Jews in the Roman World*. New York: Scribner, 1973

Harper, Robert Francis. *The Code of Hammurabi King of Babylon*. Chicago: Univ. of Chicago Press, 1904

Herodotus. Trans. by David Grene. Chicago: University of Chicago Press, 1987

The Hirsch Chumash. Translated by Daniel Haberman. New York: Feldheim / Judaica Press / Jerusalem, 2002

Interlinear Chumash. Brooklyn: Mesorah Publications, 2006

Kantor, Rabbi Mattis. *Codex Judaica*. New York: Zichron Press, 2005

Kaplan, Rabbi Aryeh. *Handbook of Jewish Thought*, Vol. 1. New York: Moznaim Publishing, 1992

Kaplan, Rabbi Aryeh. *The Living Torah*. NY/Jerusalem: Moznaim

Publishing, 1989

Kelemen, Lawrence. *To Kindle A Soul*. Southfield, MI: Targum Press, 2001

Kleiman, Yaakov. *DNA & The Bible: The Genetic Link*. Springdale, AR: Lightcatcher Books, 2010

Kook, Rabbi Abraham Isaac HaKohen. *Gold From the Land of Israel*. Trans. by Rabbi Chanan Morrison. Jerusalem/New York: Urim Publications, 2006

Lichtenstein, Aaron. The Seven Laws of Noah. Brooklyn, NY: Z.Berman Books, 1981

Locks, Gutman G. *The Spice of Torah--Gematria*. New York: Judaica Press, 1985

Menkin, Rabbi Yaakov. *Pardes Petachya*. Tel Aviv, 1936

Midrash Rabbah. Volumes I - X . London/New York: The Socino Press, 1983

Mishne Torah. Translated by Rabbi Eliyahu Touger. New York/Jerusalem: Moznaim Publishing, 2001

Mozeson, Isaac *The Origin of Speeches*, 2nd Edition. Springdale, AR: Lightcatcher Books, 2011. More information can be found on his *E-Word Dictionary* CD, updated bi-annually.

Murphy, Cullen. *Are We Rome?* New York: Houghton Mifflin Company, 2007

Newton, Isaac *The Chronology of Ancient Kingdoms Amended To which is Prefix'd, A Short Chronicle from the First Memory of Things in Europe, to the Conquest of Persia by Alexander the Great*. Whitefish, MT: Kessinger Publishing, 2004

Oren, Michael B. *Power, Faith & Fantasy*. New York/London: W.W. Norton & Co.,2007

Owen, Richard "Unearthing Rome's King." *Times* On Line UK /Oct 8th, 2007

Pedley, John Griffith. *New Light on Ancient Carthage*. Ann Arbor: University of Michigan Press, 1980

Pirke de Rabbi Rabbi Eliezer. Trans. by Gerald Friedlander. New York:

Sepher-Hermon Press, 1981

Quigley, Carroll. *Tragedy & Hope*. New York: MacMillan & Co, 1966

Rainey, Anson F. and R .Steven Notley. *The Sacred Bridge*. Jerusalem: Carta Books, 2006

Roberts, J. M. *Penguin History of the World*. London: Penguin Books, 1976

Rosenberg, Rabbi A. J. *Commentary on Book of Genesis, Vol 1*. New York: Judaica Press, 1993

Rotenberg, Rabbi Shlomo. *Am Olam: History of the Eternal Nation*. Brooklyn: Keren Pub., 1988

Sagg, H. W. F. *The Babylonians*. London: Folio Society, 1999

Sefer HaYashar. Hoboken, NJ: Yosher /KTAV Publishing House, 1993

Senor, Dan and Saul Singer. *Start-Up Nation*. New York: Twelve Books, 2009

Shulman, Eliezer. *Sequence of Events in the Old Testament*. Translated by Sarah Ledenhendler. Tel-Aviv: Ministry of Defense Publishers, 1987

Singer, Rabbi Tovia. *Let's Get Biblical*. NY/Jerusalem: RNBN Publishing, 2001

Slifkin, Nosson. *Lying for the Truth*. Southfield, MI: Targum Press, 1996

Solomon, David. *The Whole of Jewish History in One Hour*. Tel Aviv: In One Hour Publications, 2008

Spiro, Ken. *Crash Course in Jewish History*. Southfield, MI: Targum Press, 2010

The Talmud, The Steinsaltz Edition. New York: Random House, 1989

The Tanakh, Stone Edition. Edited by Rabbi Nosson Scherman. Brooklyn, NY: Mesorah Publications, Ltd., 2007

Weinberg, Rabbi Matis *Frameworks: Genesis*. Boston/Jerusalem: Foundation for Jewish Publications. 1999

The Works of Philo of Alexandria. Trans. by C. D. Yonge. Hendrickson Publishers, 1993

INDEX

Biblical References

Torah

Genesis 3:1
Genesis 6:19-20
Genesis 7:2-4
Genesis 9:1
Genesis 9:4-6
Genesis 9:25
Genesis 9:4-6
Genesis 9:8
Genesis 10:4
Genesis 10:8-12
Genesis 11:1,2
Genesis 11:32
Genesis 12:2
Genesis 14:1
Genesis 14:16- 18
Genesis 15:7-8
Genesis 15:13-16
Genesis 22:9-18
Genesis 25:23
Genesis 25:29-33
Genesis 26:34-35
Genesis 27:22
Genesis 27:27-29
Genesis 27:34-36
Genesis 28:5
Genesis 28:13-14
Genesis 28:16-17
Genesis 31:14 - 16
Genesis 32:31
Genesis 33:14
Genesis 36:1-3
Genesis 36:11
Genesis 36:15
Genesis 36:32
Exodus 4:22
Exodus 12:40
Exodus 19:6
Exodus 20:1-14
Exodus 23:13
Exodus 40:15
Numbers 24:24
Deuteronomy 12:5
Deuteronomy 26:18
Deuteronomy 28:15
Deuteronomy 30:1- 6
Deuteronomy 31:19

Prophets

Joshua 10:13
2 Samuel 1:18
Isaiah 2:16
Isaiah 23:1
Isaiah 56: 6-7
Isaiah 66:19
Jeremiah 10:9
Jeremiah 17:19
Jeremiah 29:14

Writings

For more information about Lightcatcher Books

go to

LightcatcherBooks.com

NOTES

www.ingramcontent.com/pod-product-compliance
Lightning Source LLC
LaVergne TN
LVHW091141080826
845145LV00008B/2216